11&12

LEVEL

M

Language

TABE®
MASTERY

New Readers Press®
ProLiteracy's publishing division

TABE® Mastery
Level M Language
ISBN 978-1-944057-343

Copyright © 2019 New Readers Press
New Readers Press
ProLiteracy's Publishing Division
101 Wyoming Street, Syracuse, New York 13204
www.newreaderspress.com

Printed in the United States of America
10 9 8 7 6 5 4

Proceeds from the sale of New Readers Press materials support professional
development, training, and technical assistance programs of ProLiteracy
that benefit local literacy programs in the U.S. and around the globe.

Editorial Director: Terrie Lipke
Editor: Jennifer Thompson
Cover Design: Cathi Miller
Technology Specialist: Maryellen Casey

Contents

Pretest

1. Which sentence is written correctly?

   A. We went to the park, but either the swings nor the basketball court were free.

   B. We went to the park, but neither the swings nor the basketball court were free.

   C. We went to the park, but neither the swings or the basketball court were free.

   D. We went to the park, but either the swings or the basketball court were free.

2. Read the paragraph.

   (1) The sun, which warms and lights Earth, is one of many stars in our galaxy. (2) Because of that, nobody can say for sure how many stars are in the galaxy. (3) We cannot see everything in the whole galaxy. (4) The Earth is in the Milky Way galaxy, which is a collection of stars, planets, and other space objects.

   What is the correct order of sentences for an introduction paragraph?

   A. 4, 1, 2, 3

   B. 1, 2, 4, 3

   C. 2, 1, 3, 4

   D. 4, 1, 3, 2

3. Which sentence uses a past participle?

   A. He had walked to the store for milk.

   B. He was walking to the store for milk.

   C. He would like to walk to the store for milk.

   D. He will walk to the store for milk.

4. Which sentence uses correct capitalization?

   A. My friend Stacey wants to be a Teacher.

   B. On tuesday, I am going to take the Train to New York City.

   C. My mom wants me to talk to the doctor for her.

   D. Over the weekend, we saw a Whale in the Ocean.

5. Read the paragraph.

   Summer school is not just for students who do not do well in a class, but also for students who want to get ahead or learn something new. Many schools offer interesting classes. My friend took a really cool art class. Some colleges also have special programs for high school students or adult learners. Students can focus on an area of interest they may not have time for during the school year. This can truly enhance the educational experience.

   Which sentence should be removed because it does not fit the paragraph?

   A. Many schools offer interesting classes.

   B. Students can focus on an area of interest they may not have time for during the school year.

   C. My friend took a really cool art class.

   D. Some colleges also have special programs for high school students or adult learners.

6. Read the paragraph.

> (1) I am trying to acommodate all my friends in my planning. (2) One of them cannot come on Wednesday. (3) It may be necessary to have the meeting without her. (4) Her schedule is very tight.

Which sentence contains a misspelled word?

A. 1

B. 2

C. 3

D. 4

7. Which of the following statements is an opinion?

A. Without a college education, a person can't be successful.

B. There are many different breeds of dogs.

C. The United States has coasts on the Atlantic and Pacific oceans.

D. A healthy diet includes fruits and vegetables.

8. Which sentence is written correctly?

A. My doctor said that "You need to eat healthy foods".

B. "This is going to be a long day". My co-worker said.

C. My boss said, "Everyone has to come to the meeting."

D. My friend said, "tomorrow I am going on vacation."

9. Which sentence is written in a more formal style?

A. I was chilling at the park.

B. I didn't have anything to do this weekend.

C. I relaxed after I got home from work.

D. A few of us were going out.

10. Which sentence is punctuated correctly?

A. I had a headache, so I stayed home.

B. Because, of the parade, the streets were blocked.

C. I watched a fun show, after school yesterday.

D. Tim yells, when he is angry.

11. Which is the best topic sentence for an explanatory essay?

A. Owning a house is better than renting.

B. There are benefits to buying a condominium instead of a house.

C. Renters do not have to pay for repairs or upkeep.

D. It is important to look at the pluses and minuses when deciding to rent or buy a place to live.

12. Read the sentence. Choose the correct definition for the underlined word.

> I wrote a <u>chronology</u> for my history paper. Then I drew a timeline from it.

A. a summary of important events

B. a list of events in the order that they happened

C. an outline of a research project

D. a proposal for an essay

13. Which sentence is written logically and correctly?

A. Sheila will graduate Sunday, otherwise, she will go to a party after.

B. Marlin went to a baseball game, nevertheless, he had a fun afternoon.

C. Carly missed her bus, therefore, she was late to her appointment.

D. Henry smiled and said he would do the job, although he really wanted to do it.

14. Which sentence is written correctly?

A. The rainbow during the storm.

B. When the war began, people fled their homes.

C. Was time to leave.

D. Returning the ladder to my neighbor.

15. Read the paragraph.

> (1) A way to do this is to have the child pick something to work toward. (2) Put the money in a savings account. (3) As a result, they learn how to reach long-term goals. (4) Children should learn the importance of saving. (5) They can get paid for chores or odd jobs for friends and neighbors. (6) Then, when they reach the goal, they can spend the money.

What is the correct order of sentences for a supporting paragraph?

A. 4, 1, 5, 2, 6, 3

B. 6, 3, 4, 2, 1, 5

C. 2, 6, 4, 5, 1, 3

D. 4, 1, 2, 3, 6, 5

16. Read the paragraph.

> (1) Yesterday, Tasha and I went to the office together. (2) We drove in slow traffic. (3) We saw a lot of people that were doing other things while they drove. (4) One person was even brushing his teeth.

Which sentence contains an incorrect relative pronoun?

A. 1

B. 2

C. 3

D. 4

17. Which sentence is the best choice for an explanatory English paper?

    A. The book was good and had a fun ending.

    B. I did not like this book because it was sad.

    C. The author used descriptive language to support the plot.

    D. The author's other books are better.

18. Which sentence is written correctly?

    A. Their going to make sure the house is spotless.

    B. There dog barks all day and night.

    C. Your sure you want to go to the play?

    D. If you're driving a long distance, you should take a break.

19. Read the paragraph.

    First off, a plan allows you to take logical steps to reach a goal. It also helps you remember everything you need to do and to break it into manageable pieces.

    The paragraph is missing an introduction. Which of these would best introduce the topic?

    A. To achieve a goal, it is best to have a detailed plan.

    B. Planning takes a lot of work and time.

    C. Everyone needs to have a goal in life.

    D. If you are not going to plan, you won't reach your goals.

20. Which sentence is written correctly?

    A. Kelsey, is running errands, to the grocery store, and the bank.

    B. Stephan likes to run, and jump, but he cannot catch well.

    C. Mavis, will you buy potatoes, corn, and hamburger buns?

    D. Dante has to, mow the lawn, walk the dog, and start dinner.

21. Read the sentence.

    Playing a musical instrument can be rewarding, but it requires many hours of practice.

    Which quotation best supports the statement?

    A. "I picked up the guitar and just started to play."

    B. "I spent hours practicing the piano before I could play this song."

    C. "There's no reason to take music lessons, just play."

    D. "Anyone can bang on a drum and be in a band."

Read the paragraph. Then answer questions 22–24.

Spiders vs. Insects

Many people think spiders are insects, but they are not. Spiders are <u>arachnids</u> that build webs to catch insects. Arachnids have eight legs and their bodies have two <u>segments</u>, or parts. Insects have six legs and three body segments. Insects have <u>compound</u> eyes, which have many small parts that create an image, and arachnids have simple eyes. They also do not have wings or <u>antennae</u>, the long, wiry parts that help insects feel.

22. Which sentence uses the word *arachnids* correctly?

   A. When arachnids fly around, they can look scary.

   B. Arachnids use eight legs to crawl around.

   C. When arachnids use their antennae, they are feeling their environment.

   D. Arachnids use their compound eyes to see the world.

23. Which sentence uses the word *segments* correctly?

   A. Arachnids don't have segments, so they cannot fly.

   B. Arachnids and insects both use their segments to feel the world.

   C. Arachnids have two segments that make up their bodies.

   D. Insects use their segments to find food.

24. Which sentence uses the word *antennae* correctly?

   A. Insects have antennae that they use to feel the spaces around them.

   B. A spider needs antennae to help build a web.

   C. Antennae help insects see better when they fly.

   D. Without antennae, arachnids would have trouble crawling.

25. Which sentence correctly uses an example of dialect?

   A. Do y'all want more nachos when I get up?

   B. Let's all go to the movies tomorrow.

   C. I hope he buys that house.

   D. The sun came out after it rained.

26. Which sentence is written correctly?

   A. The woman on the train was reading "The New York Times."

   B. My favorite book is "Anna Karenina" by Leo Tolstoy.

   C. My history teacher assigned us the chapter *The Ottoman Empire* for homework.

   D. I read the book *The Hunger Games* by Suzanne Collins before I saw the movie.

27. Which sentence is written correctly?

   A. To the store to buy a new dress.

   B. In the car with DeeDee.

   C. Because the power went out in the storm.

   D. When I finish my work, I can go.

28. Read the sentence.

> One reason to travel by airplane is that it is faster.

Which is the best choice for the next sentence?

A. However, it is safer than some people think.

B. Otherwise, it is safer than some people think.

C. Secondly, it is safer than some people think.

D. Therefore, it is safer than some people think.

29. Read the opinion statement.

> Studying literature is a necessary part of education.

What is a logical supporting reason for this opinion?

A. Literature helps students learn other viewpoints.

B. Literature is easier than math or science.

C. Literature gives students a break from real subjects.

D. Literature is often made into fun movies.

30. Which sentence contains a modal auxiliary?

A. They had gone shopping before school.

B. The nurse will give the patient her medicine.

C. The chairperson of the committee will be calling for a vote.

D. The lawyer must file the brief by Tuesday.

31. Read the paragraph.

> (1) Dylan wanted to buy a new computer. (2) He asked his dad for his advice. (3) His dad told him he should do research first. (4) Dylan took his dad's advice and then bought a new computer.

Which sentence contains a prepositional phrase?

A. 1

B. 2

C. 3

D. 4

32. Which sentence is written correctly?

A. Serena and I plan to go to the Lake to go for a swim on Thursday.

B. Next year, I will take algebra, English, American History, and biology.

C. The Chairperson of the Math club scheduled a practice for the morning.

D. Would you help me study for my European history test on Tuesday, Father?

33. Which sentence uses correct spelling?

A. It is a privilege to be here on this occasion.

B. I am embarrased that I have so much trouble with grammer.

C. Calvin receeved an email confirming his travel skedule.

D. I am truly surprised the award is so miniscule.

34. Read the sentence.

Soccer may be the most popular sport in the world.

Which fact best supports this argument?

A. Baseball is probably the second most popular sport.

B. More than 3.5 billion people watched some of the 2018 World Cup.

C. In most countries outside the United States, the sport is called football.

D. The U.S. women's team has won four World Cups.

35. Read the paragraph.

(1) When Carlos gets up in the morning he gets dressed. (2) Next, he eats breakfast. (3) His mom usually makes eggs, toast, and bacon. (4) Finally, he brushes his teeth and goes to school.

Which sentence is written incorrectly?

A. 1

B. 2

C. 3

D. 4

36. Which sentence is written using formal language?

A. My dog Spike would not go on her usual two-mile walk.

B. We can get that done whenever.

C. Wanna get some snacks with me?

D. Melanie doesn't want to go to the party.

37. Read the sentence.

Sylvia's writing is difficult to read because she has dysgraphia.

What does the word *dysgraphia* mean?

A. a leg injury

B. a medical condition that affects handwriting

C. a bad grip

D. vision problems

38. Read the paragraph.

Reading Music

Learning to read music is like learning a new language. The letters, or notes, are written on five lines. The five lines are called a staff. The first mark on a staff is a clef. The clef indicates how high the pitch of the music is. Then, the notes are written on or between the lines. The note head, or the O-shaped part, can be filled-in or blank. That tells the musician how long to hold the note.

Which sentence uses the word *staff* correctly?

A. Musicians look at the staff to tell them how long to hold a note.

B. The staff tells musicians how high the pitch of the music is.

C. Musical notes are written on a staff with five lines.

D. The staff can be filled in or blank.

39. Read the sentence.

    Doctors say people should eat less sugar.

    Which is the best choice for the next sentence?

    A. Nevertheless, many people eat more than doctors recommend.

    B. Therefore, many people eat more than doctors recommend.

    C. Also, many people eat more than doctors recommend.

    D. Secondly, many people eat more than doctors recommend.

40. Read the sentence.

    Carmen loves the summertime; _____, she sunburns easily.

    Which relationship word best fits in the blank?

    A. therefore

    B. however

    C. moreover

    D. similarly

41. Which sentence is punctuated correctly?

    A. "My presentation will take about 10 minutes" Eden said.

    B. The store clerk said that, "My new shoes would be ready next week."

    C. "I asked you four times to clean your room!" my mother exclaimed.

    D. "According to Lou, New York has the best pizza."

42. Which choice best completes the sentence?

    My favorite book when I was younger was _____.

    A. "Green Eggs and Ham" by Dr. Seuss.

    B. *Green Eggs and Ham* by *Dr. Seuss*.

    C. *Green Eggs and Ham* by Dr. Seuss.

    D. "Green Eggs and Ham" by "Dr. Seuss."

43. Read the paragraph.

    Tsunamis, also called tidal waves, can be very dangerous. They are caused by earthquakes or volcanic eruptions under the seas and cause huge waves. Tsunamis most often happen in the Pacific Ocean, but they can occur in other places.

    What would be a good addition to this paragraph?

    A. a list of other ocean dangers

    B. a phone number for an emergency shelter

    C. a sentence telling why tsunamis are dangerous

    D. a prediction of when the next tsunami will be

44. Which sentence is written correctly?

    A. Sura will want to go to the ice-skating rink yesterday.

    B. When his mother called, Diego had been walking to the store.

    C. Larissa had went back to college after working for a year.

    D. Before the thunder, the rain had began.

45. Which sentence is written correctly?

    A. Abel went at the football game with his friends.

    B. We rented a car to drive on the city.

    C. The children liked going through the slide at the park.

    D. Samantha had an itch on her nose.

46. Read the paragraph.

    (1) Winter sports can be a lot of fun if your dressed warmly. (2) If you like the occassional fast ride, you may like downhill skiing. (3) You may like snowboarding to. (4) Another choice is cross-country skiing, where there are flat areas and you can go at your own pace.

    Which sentence is written correctly?

    A. 1

    B. 2

    C. 3

    D. 4

47. Which is the strongest topic sentence for an opinion essay on social media?

    A. Participating in social media has more negatives than positives.

    B. There are many different types of social media these days.

    C. Social media has pluses and minuses depending on how it is used.

    D. Social media companies are very profitable for their owners.

48. Which sentence uses an example of dialect?

    A. When I was a child, my grandma always let me drink pop.

    B. "Thanks for the present," Brad said.

    C. My brother-in-law is my wife's favorite sibling.

    D. I think Cajun food is the most delicious cuisine.

49. Which sentence is written correctly?

    A. The firefighter, who saved the cat from the tree, got a reward from its owner.

    B. The boss, which hired my friend, also gave me a raise.

    C. My friend has a parrot who says, "Hello, partner," when I visit.

    D. Ronaldo is the soccer player that I like the most.

50. What is the purpose of an introduction in an informational essay?

    A. It tells the writer's opinion on the topic.

    B. It lists the facts the writer will use to explain the topic.

    C. It gives background and a topic sentence.

    D. It offers a problem and solution.

Answers begin on page 104.

Pretest Action Plan

Highlight all the questions that you answered correctly. Count the number of correct answers and write that in the second column. The results will help identify the skills that need improvement.

Questions	Number Correct	Skills	Pages
14, 27	_____ / 2	Write Complete Sentences	16–17
16, 49	_____ / 2	Use Relative Pronouns and Adverbs	18
18, 46	_____ / 2	Use Frequently Confused Words	18–19
1, 31, 45	_____ / 3	Use Conjunctions, Prepositions, and Interjections	23–25
3, 30, 44	_____ / 3	Form Verb Tenses	25–27
4, 32	_____ / 2	Capitalize Correctly	33
26, 42	_____ / 2	Write Titles of Works	33–34
6, 33	_____ / 2	Spell Correctly	34–35
10, 20, 35	_____ / 3	Use Commas	39–41
8, 41	_____ / 2	Punctuate Quotations	41
5, 36	_____ / 2	Modify Sentences	45–46
25, 48	_____ / 2	Identify Dialects in Fiction	47–48
12, 37	_____ / 2	Determine Definitions	59–61
22, 23, 24, 38	_____ / 4	Use Topic Words	65–66
13, 28, 39, 40	_____ / 4	Use Relationship Words	71
7, 15, 19, 29, 34, 47	_____ / 6	Write Opinion Pieces	79–80
11, 50	_____ / 2	Introduce Informative/Explanatory Texts	85
2, 9, 17, 21, 43	_____ / 5	Write Informative/Explanatory Texts	86–87
Total	_____ **/ 50**		

UNIT 1

Standard English Conventions

This unit will cover the following topics:

- Following grammar rules
- Using correct sentence structure
- Following capitalization and spelling rules
- Using correct punctuation
- Using varied sentence styles

Alejandro works in a call center for a large company that sells outdoor lawn equipment. He has been doing the same job for about five years and really likes his boss, James.

Recently, James told Alejandro there was a chance for him to get a promotion. In the new job, Alejandro would have to respond to written messages and e-mails from customers. Alejandro was very excited about the opportunity. He was also worried that he did not have the basic skills to write clearly in response to the customers.

Alejandro began to learn the rules of grammar and practiced using correct punctuation and spelling by writing letters to his family. After a few weeks, he was able to write a letter to James asking for the new job. As a result of learning and practicing the rules of grammar, Alejandro got a new job and a raise.

Language is the way we communicate with one another. Following certain rules helps to make our language more clear and professional. With good language skills, we can create better opportunities for ourselves.

Follow Grammar Rules

Vocabulary

- complete sentence
- subject
- predicate
- fragment
- run-on sentence
- relative pronoun
- relative adverb

Think

In some sentences, the subject is understood. That means the subject does not actually appear in the sentence, but we know what it is. Consider this sentence: "Stop!" Here, the understood subject is *you*, and the predicate is *stop*.

Learning Goals

In this lesson, you will learn how to tell a complete sentence from an incomplete one. You will learn how to find whether a group of words has a subject and a predicate. You will learn how to put adjectives in the right order. You will learn about sentence fragments, run-on sentences, relative pronouns, and relative adverbs. You will also learn about some frequently confused words.

Learn the Skill

Grammar rules help us communicate. They guide us to use the right words at the right time and in the right context. They teach us how to place words in an understandable order and how to use punctuation to avoid confusion. Following grammar rules in class and at work will help you communicate clearly and professionally.

Example 1

A Complete Sentence Has a Subject and a Predicate

A complete sentence has a subject and a predicate. The subject is the noun on which the sentence is focused. The predicate contains the main verb in the sentence and usually all the words following the main verb. The predicate provides information about the subject, such as what the subject is, what it is like, or what it is doing.

Look at the subjects and predicates in these sentences:

Subject	Predicate
We	like apples.
Calvin and I	like apples.
Everyone in the factory	likes apples.
Everyone in the factory	likes to eat apples and oranges every day.

If a sentence is missing a subject or a predicate, it is called a **fragment**, or an incomplete sentence.

For example, this fragment is missing a subject: *Likes apples!*

This fragment is missing a predicate: *Everyone in the factory.*

A **run-on sentence** contains two or more sentences that are not correctly joined together. For example: *We like apples they like oranges.*

You can often fix a run-on by breaking it into two sentences, adding a semicolon, or a adding a comma and conjunction (*and*, *but*, etc.) For example:

> *We like apples. They like oranges.*
> *We like apples; they like oranges.*
> *We like apples, and they like oranges.*

Avoid using fragments and run-ons in formal writing.

Example 2

Adjectives Should Be Ordered Within Sentences According to Conventional Patterns

You will sometimes need or want to use one or more adjectives in a sentence to help you describe something. In such cases, be sure to place your adjectives in the correct order. This may come naturally to you. For example, your ear may be able to tell you that the first sentence here sounds more natural than the second sentence:

> *I have a big yellow car.*
> *I have a yellow big car.*

When you are using several adjectives, it will help to check your writing against this order:

quantity, opinion, size, age, shape, color, origin, material, and purpose

For example: *I have three incredible, new, red, Italian race cars.* (quantity, opinion, new, color, origin, purpose)

Check for Errors

Use the relative pronoun *which*, with commas, for nonessential information. Use *that*, without commas, for essential information. For example: *The car in the driveway, <u>which</u> is my brother's, has a flat tire. The car <u>that</u> my brother drives has a flat tire.*

Check for Errors

If your writing has incorrect words, your readers might wonder whether you know what you're writing about. Be sure to check for commonly confused words before you submit or post any written work.

Example 3

Relative Pronouns and Adverbs Help Provide More Information About a Person or Thing

Relative pronouns (*who*, *whose*, *whom*, *which*, and *that*) help give more information about a person or a thing. When commas are used with these pronouns, the information is considered nonessential (unnecessary). For example: *Tanya, who lives next door, is a plumber.* Here, the clause between the commas is not necessary for telling us which person is a plumber. Even without that clause, we know that Tanya is a plumber.

Now, look at this sentence: *The woman who lives next door is a plumber.* Here, the clause *who lives next door* is necessary for telling us which woman is a plumber. This is why we do not place commas around it. The clause is essential.

Relative adverbs (*where*, *when*, and *why*) also help give more information, usually about a place, time, or reason. For example: *Lee lives in the city <u>where</u> he was born. He started working <u>when</u> he was 12 years old. The nice weather is the main reason <u>why</u> he still lives there.*

Commas are used much less often with relative adverbs than with relative pronouns. Still, you will sometimes see them. Here is an example: *Lee started working in 2005, when he was 12 years old. Lee lives in San Diego, <u>where</u> he was born.*

As with relative pronouns, commas are used with relative adverbs to set off nonessential information.

Example 4

Understanding Frequently Confused Words Can Help You Communicate

Here is a chart with some commonly confused words. Some of these are homophones, meaning they sound exactly the same. Others sound similar to each other or have similar spellings. Knowing the meanings and spellings of these words can help you appear more knowledgeable and professional in the classroom or workplace.

Use this chart to help you use these commonly confused words.

Word	Meaning	Example Sentence
accept	to agree to receive or do something	*I did not accept the low salary I was offered.*
except	not including	*I like all kinds of jobs except ones that require a lot of time at a computer.*
affect	to change or make a difference to something	*The weather can affect my mood.*
effect	a result	*Sunshine has a good effect on my mood.*

Word	Meaning	Example Sentence
brake	a device used to stop something	The cyclist needed to repair the front brake on her bike.
break	1) a pause 2) to separate into pieces	1) The workers take a break every two hours. 2) You will break that window if you keep tapping it with that hammer.
ensure	to make sure that something will happen	I can't ensure that tomorrow will be sunny.
insure	to provide insurance for something	Expensive cars cost a lot to insure.
it's	it is	It's too cold to work outside today.
its	of or belonging to something	That bike is nice, but its wheels are flat.
than	a word used to compare things	I would rather work holidays than weekends.
then	at that time	I'm going to work until 5:00 and then go fishing.
they're	they are	I love these shoes. They're my favorites.
their	possessive form of they	Their house is older than our house.
there	indicates location	I like to take my break at that park bench over there.
though	however	I don't like to work weekends, though I will if I have to.
thorough	careful or complete	I gave the engine a thorough inspection.
through	into or out of	I ran through the woods.
threw	past tense of throw	I threw my garbage in the trash can.
thru	nonstandard spelling of through	I would rather work at the drive-thru window than in the kitchen.
two	the number after one	I'll be working two jobs this summer.
too	also; in addition to	My brother is a nurse. I want to be one too.
to	in the direction of	Let's go to the beach!
your	of or belonging to you	What is your name?
you're	you are	I think you're going to pass this class.

Think

If you are not sure how to pronounce a word, use the internet. Many online dictionaries provide pronunciations of words.

Think

Relative pronouns and adverbs are not always necessary. For example, Sentence 6 on this page could be rewritten like this: *She'll use the bike to commute around the city her job is in.*

Guided Practice

Read the paragraph and make corrections where needed. Then explain the reason for each correction.

1. (1) My sister Francine had a job interview yesterday, she is trying to get hired as an IT specialist. (2) Francine which is five years older than me has been working on computers since she was seven years old. (3) Loves to work on computers! (4) Francine is looking for a job that pays more then her current job. (5) If she gets this job, she's going to buy herself a hybrid, blue, new bicycle. (6) She'll use the bike to commute around the city when her job is.

    _____

    _____

    _____

    _____

    _____

    _____

    Answers: (1) . . . yesterday. She . . .—run-on sentence (2) Francine, who is five years older than me, has—relative pronoun error (3) She loves—sentence fragment (4) . . . pays more than her—word-choice error (5) . . . new, blue, hybrid bicycle.—adjective word-order error (6) . . . city where her . . .—relative adverb error

Independent Practice

Choose the best answer for each question about the correct use of grammar.

2. Which of these is a run-on sentence?

    A. I have to wake up early tomorrow, traffic will be bad.

    B. I have to wake up early tomorrow because traffic will be bad.

    C. I have to wake up early tomorrow. Traffic will be bad.

    D. I have to wake up early tomorrow; traffic will be bad.

3. Which of these is a complete sentence?

    A. Need to take the bus.

    B. Will take the bus to work tomorrow.

    C. My friend and I will take the bus.

    D. My friend and I.

4. Which of these shows adjectives in proper order?

    A. three silk, large, old, round cushions

    B. silk, large, old, round, three cushions

    C. large, old, round, three, silk cushions

    D. three large, old, round, silk cushions

5. Which sentence shows a correct usage of relative pronouns?

    A. I like dogs that don't bark.

    B. I like dogs which don't bark.

    C. I like dogs whom don't bark.

    D. I like dogs, that don't bark.

6. Which sentence shows correct usage of relative adverbs?

    A. I remember the time, where we traveled to Spain.

    B. I remember the time which we traveled to Spain.

    C. I remember the time, which we traveled to Spain.

    D. I remember the time when we traveled to Spain.

7. Which sentence shows correct usage of frequently confused words?

    A. Studying can help insure that you'll pass the test.

    B. Studying will help you learn all the material too.

    C. You should take a 15-minute brake from studying.

    D. Go threw all the practice questions when studying.

Test Tip

Check if part of a sentence can stand alone as a separate sentence, such as this from question 2: *traffic will be bad.* If it can stand alone, then you probably need more than just a comma to connect it to the rest of the sentence.

Lesson Review

In this lesson, you learned to

- write complete sentences;
- correct fragments and run-ons;
- correctly order adjectives in sentences;
- recognize and use relative pronouns and adverbs; and
- identify and use frequently confused words.

Correct fragments and run-ons and identify correctly ordered adjectives.

8. Read the samples below. Which one contains a sentence fragment?

   A. My college offers many practical courses, such as welding, plumbing, and coding.

   B. My college offers many practical courses. Such as welding, plumbing, and coding.

   C. My college offers many practical courses. These include welding, plumbing, and coding.

   D. My college offers many practical courses, among which are welding, plumbing, and coding.

9. Read the sentence.

   In my free time I like to go hiking, my wife prefers to read novels.

   Which sentence corrects the run-on?

   A. In my free time I like to go hiking my wife prefers to read novels.

   B. In my free time I like to go hiking with my wife prefers to read novels.

   C. In my free time I like to go hiking. My wife prefers to read novels.

   D. In my free time I like to go hiking; but my wife prefers to read novels.

10. Which sentence orders adjectives correctly?

   A. The workers placed new, several, large, iron support rods in the cement.

   B. The workers placed large, new, iron, support, several rods in the cement.

   C. The workers placed several large, new, support, iron rods in the cement.

   D. The workers placed several large, new, iron, support rods in the cement.

Recognize and use relative pronouns and adverbs.

11. Read the sentences below. Choose three that use relative pronouns correctly.

   A. My manager doesn't like workers who show up to work late.

   B. My manager doesn't like workers, who show up to work late.

   C. My manager, who never shows up late, is strict.

   D. My manager, that never shows up late, is strict.

   E. My job, which is the easiest one I've ever had, doesn't pay well.

Identify and use frequently confused words.

12. Read the sentence.

   The children can't except the fact that there behavior effects how their treated.

   Which sentence corrects the commonly confused words?

   A. The children can't accept the fact that they're behavior effects how there treated.

   B. The children can't accept the fact that their behavior affects how they're treated.

   C. The children can't except the fact that their behavior effects how there treated.

   D. The children can't except the fact that there behavior affects how their treated.

Answers begin on page 105.

LESSON 2

Use Correct Sentence Structure

Learning Goals

In this lesson, you will learn how to use correct sentence structures. This includes understanding, identifying, and using conjunctions, prepositions, interjections, correlative conjunctions, prepositional phrases, modal auxiliaries, past participles, and several verb tenses.

Vocabulary

- conjunction
- preposition
- interjection
- modal auxiliary

Learn the Skill

The basic sentence structure of English is Subject – Verb – Object (S-V-O). For example: *Joe likes pizza.* As you learned in Lesson 1, *Joe* is the subject and *likes pizza* is the predicate. Remember that the predicate includes the main verb of the sentence and usually any words that follow that verb. In this case, the predicate is made up of the verb *likes* and the object *pizza*.

However, sentences often contain more than just a subject, verb, and object. It is important to understand how conjunctions can connect different parts of a sentence, how prepositions can add important information, and how modals can add shades of meaning.

Example 1

Use Conjunctions, Prepositions, and Interjections

Conjunctions can connect sentences, clauses, phrases, or words. (A clause is a group of words that has a subject-verb relationship. A phrase is a group of words that function together.) Here are some common conjunctions: *and, but, or, nor, yet, so, for, because, although, though, if,* and *since.*

Here are some example sentences:

Every morning I eat apples, bananas, or oranges. (connects words)
I live in Denver, and my sister lives in Santa Fe. (connects clauses/sentences)
Although I love literature, I studied nursing in college. (connects clauses)

Prepositions are words that give more information about things like time or location. Some of the most common prepositions are: *of, in, to, into, for, with, on, at, from, by, between, before, after, below,* and *about.*

Interjections don't really serve a grammatical function. Instead, they can convey moods or feelings. This means they can be useful at work, especially when spoken. For example:

Hey, watch out for that broken glass!

Well, I guess you're right. I should have handled that situation differently.

Test Tip

Correlative conjunctions are set pairs. Memorize them! You might see one half of the pair in a question and the other half in the answer. For example, if *not only* appears in a question, *but also* will likely appear in the right answer.

Prepositions usually come before the nouns that they modify. For example:

Place: *The book is <u>on</u> the <u>table</u>. The idea is <u>in</u> my <u>head</u>. The pipe runs <u>under</u> the <u>sidewalk</u>.*
Time: *Let's meet <u>at</u> <u>six o'clock</u>. The movie starts <u>in</u> <u>15 minutes</u>. My shift goes <u>from</u> <u>morning until night</u>.*

An **interjection**, or exclamation, is a word, phrase, or clause that shows a strong feeling. Common interjections include: *ah, hey, oh, ow, really, well*

Interjections can be part of a sentence or stand alone. For example:

<u>Hey</u>, that's my car!
<u>Well</u>, we could go see a movie.
<u>Ouch</u>! That hurt.

Interjections are more common in spoken English or informal writing than in formal writing.

Example 2

Explain the Purpose of Correlative Conjunctions

Correlative conjunctions consist of two or more words used together to connect parts of a sentence. For example:

I can work <u>either</u> nights <u>or</u> days.
<u>Neither</u> rain <u>nor</u> snow can prevent me from getting to work on time.
I can work <u>both</u> Saturdays <u>and</u> Sundays.
I can work <u>not only</u> Sundays <u>but also</u> holidays.

Example 3

Identify, Explain, and Use Prepositional Phrases

All prepositional phrases begin with a preposition and end with the object of that preposition, which is usually a noun or pronoun. Some prepositional phrases also have modifiers. Below are some examples.

preposition + noun – <u>at home</u>
preposition + modifiers + noun – <u>at the little red schoolhouse</u>
preposition + pronoun – <u>with you</u>
preposition + modifiers + pronoun – <u>with more of us</u>

Prepositional phrases usually function as adjectives or adverbs. As adjectives, prepositional phrases will answer the question *Which one?* For example:

The car <u>in the parking lot</u> is mine. (Which car? The one in the parking lot.)

As adverbs, prepositional phrases will answer the questions *Where? When?* or *Why?* For example:

My car is in the parking lot. (Where is it? In the parking lot.)
Let's go home at three o'clock. (When should we go home? At three o'clock.)
I am tired from a long, hard day. (Why are you tired? From working long and hard.)

Example 4

Identify and Explain the Purpose of Modal Auxiliaries

Modal auxiliaries are used with other verbs to give different shades of meaning to those verbs. The main modal auxiliaries are *can, could, may, might, must, shall, should, will,* and *would.*

Consider the different shades of meaning in these sentences:
I eat. I can eat. I might eat. I must eat. I should eat.

Modal auxiliaries generally express these things:

	Example sentences
Probability	I *might* | *may* | *could* | *should* pass this test if I study for it. I *can't* pass this test, even if I study for it. I *should* have passed the test because I studied for it. I *must* have passed the test because I studied so hard for it.
Ability	He *can* speak eight languages. He *could* play the piano when he was three years old.
Requests	*Could* | *Would* | *Can* | *Will* you help me paint my house?
Offers and Invitations	*Can* I help you with that? I *can* | *could* drive you to work if you need a ride.
Permission	*Can* | *Could* | *May* we take a break? Yes, you *can* | *may* take a break.
Suggestions	You *should* apply for that job. We *should* | *could* have dinner after work.
Obligations	All workers *must* wear boots. Employees *cannot* use phones while working.

Example 5

Identify and Correctly Use Past Participles

Past participles are verbs used with *have / has / had* and *were / was*. With regular verbs, the past participle will have an *-ed* ending. Here are some example sentences:

Test Tip

Some prepositions are closely associated with specific verbs. For example: *look at, glance at, stare at, smile at, laugh at, approve of, consist of, dream of, think of, hope for, look for, wait for, wish for.* Look for these pairs when you're taking a test.

I have used this app many times.
He has needed some help for several hours.
He was helped by many people.

With irregular verbs, the form of the past participle must be memorized. Here are some examples:

Infinitive	Simple past	Past participle
be	was/were	been
become	became	become
begin	began	begun
break	broke	broken
choose	chose	chosen
come	came	come
do	did	done
draw	drew	drawn
drive	drove	driven
eat	ate	eaten
fall	fell	fallen
fly	flew	flown
forget	forgot	forgotten
get	got	got or gotten
give	gave	given
go	went	gone
grow	grew	grown
know	knew	known
ride	rode	ridden
run	ran	run
see	saw	seen
steal	stole	stolen
sing	sang	sung
speak	spoke	spoken
take	took	taken
throw	threw	thrown
wear	wore	worn
write	wrote	written

Example 6

Identify and Correctly Use Past, Present, Future, Progressive, and Perfect Verb Tenses

English has 12 verb tenses. We will look at some of them here.

Lesson 2 | Use Correct Sentence Structure

The following chart gives example sentences and brief explanations (in parentheses) for each tense. Example sentences have one regular verb (*work*) and one irregular verb (*write*).

	Past	Present	Future
Simple	I <u>worked</u> | <u>wrote</u> yesterday. (past habit or completed action)	I <u>work</u> | <u>write</u> every Monday. (habit)	I <u>will work</u> | <u>will write</u> tomorrow. (future action or condition)
Progressive	I <u>was working</u> | <u>was writing</u> yesterday afternoon. (past action in progress)	I <u>am working</u> | <u>am writing</u> now. (current action in progress)	I <u>will be working</u> | <u>will be writing</u> tomorrow afternoon. (future action in progress)
Perfect	I <u>had worked</u> | <u>had written</u> for three hours when you called me yesterday. (completed past action that happened before another action)	I <u>have worked</u> | <u>have written</u> for many hours on this project. (past action that continues through the present)	I <u>will have worked</u> | <u>will have written</u> for over 80 hours on this project by next Friday. (action that will be completed before another action or time)

It is important to understand and use proper tenses with both regular and irregular verbs.

The explanations in the table describe how these tenses are commonly used. These tenses can be used in several other ways.

© New Readers Press. All rights reserved.

Unit 1 Standard English Conventions   27

Check for Errors

Pay special attention to modals combined with perfect-tense verbs. A common mistake is to use *of* instead of *have*. This is because the contraction for *have* (*must've*, *could've*, etc.) sounds like *of*. So, this is wrong: "I should *of* known that." This is right: "I should *have* known that."

Think

We use the preposition *in* with months ("in June") and years ("in 1999"), but we use *on* with specific dates ("on June 13").

Guided Practice

Read this paragraph. Make corrections where needed. Then write the reason for each correction. Look for errors involving conjunctions, prepositions, interjections, modal auxiliaries, and verb tenses.

1. (1) Yesterday had been my birthday. (2) I was born in June 13, 1999. (3) My manager said she would buy me either pizza, ice cream, and cake for lunch. (4) I told her I could like some pizza. (5) By the time work finished, I had ate the entire pizza. (6) Wow, am I full!

    _____

    _____

    _____

    _____

    _____

    Answers: (1) Yesterday was my birthday.—verb tense error (2) I was born on—preposition error (3) or cake—correlative conjunction error (4) I would like—modal auxiliary error (5) I had eaten—past participle error (6) no error

Independent Practice

Choose the best answer for each question about the correct use of grammar.

2. Which sentence has a conjunction?

   A. I was late for work because my car broke down.

   B. My car trouble caused me to be late for work.

   C. My car trouble made me late for work.

   D. I was fifteen minutes late for work today.

3. Which sentence uses a correlative conjunction correctly?

   A. We can speak neither English or Chinese.

   B. We can speak not only English but also Chinese.

   C. We can speak either English nor Chinese.

   D. We can speak both English or Chinese.

4. Which sentence has a prepositional phrase?

   A. My work clothes were expensive.

   B. My work clothes need washing.

   C. My work clothes are dirty.

   D. My work clothes are in my car.

5. Which choice has the best use of a modal auxiliary?

   A. I don't know where Letricia is. She can be in her office.

   B. I don't know where Letricia is. She might be in her office.

   C. I don't know where Letricia is. She shall be in her office.

   D. I don't know where Letricia is. She would be in her office.

6. Which sentence uses a past participle correctly?

   A. I have chosen to study accounting.

   B. I have chose to study accounting.

   C. I have choose to study accounting.

   D. I have choice to study accounting.

7. Which sentence uses the progressive verb tense correctly?

   A. I will be listening to podcasts at work tomorrow.

   B. I have listened to many podcasts at work.

   C. I am listening to podcasts at work today.

   D. I listened to podcasts at work yesterday.

Think

Verbs connected to modal auxiliaries are always in their basic form. You never add -s, -ed, or anything else. So you write "he / she / it moves" but "he / she / it can move," or "he / she / it should move."

Lesson Review

In this lesson, you learned to

- identify the correct use of conjunctions, prepositions, and interjections;
- identify and explain the purpose of correlative conjunctions;
- identify, explain, and use prepositional phrases;
- identify and explain the purpose of modal auxiliaries;
- identify and correctly use past participles; and
- identify and correctly use past, present, future, progressive, and perfect verb tenses.

Identify the correct use of conjunctions, prepositions, and interjections.

8. Read the sentences. Which sentence uses conjunctions, prepositions, and interjections correctly?

   A. My counselor thinks I should study nursing or radiology. I told her I am going into another field.

   B. My counselor thinks I should study radiology. Well, I am going into another field.

   C. My counselor thinks I should study nursing or radiology. Well, I am going into another field.

   D. My counselor thinks I should study nursing or radiology. But I am going into another field.

Identify and explain the purpose of correlative conjunctions.

9. Read the sentences below. Choose the two that use correlative conjunctions correctly.

   A. With every meal, I'm always sure to eat both fruits and vegetables.

   B. I refuse to eat either fruits or vegetables with my breakfasts.

   C. With every meal, I'm always sure to eat both fruits or vegetables.

   D. I refuse to eat not only fruits yet also vegetables with my breakfasts.

Identify, explain, and use prepositional phrases.

10. Read the sentence.

    We are going to paint the interior of that house.

    Choose the correct explanation of a sentence part.

    A. "We are going" is a prepositional phrase. It functions as an adjective because it answers the question *When?*

    B. "To paint the" is a prepositional phrase. It functions as an adjective because it answers the question *Why?*

    C. "Of that house" is a prepositional phrase. It functions as an adverb because it answers the question *Where?*

    D. "That house" is a prepositional phrase. It functions as an adverb because it answers the question *When?*

Identify and explain the purpose of modal auxiliaries.

11. Read the sentence.

    At my office, we can have up to 60 minutes for lunch.

    Choose the best explanation of the sentence.

    A. "Have" is a modal auxiliary. It gives a sense of obligation.

    B. "Have" is a modal auxiliary. It gives a sense of permission.

    C. "Can" is a modal auxiliary. It gives a sense of obligation.

    D. "Can" is a modal auxiliary. It gives a sense of permission.

Identify and correctly use past participles.

12. Which sentence uses a past participle correctly?

    A. Before I turned in my report, I had wrote several different versions of it.

    B. Before I turned in my report, I wrote several different versions of it.

    C. Before I turned in my report, I had written several different versions of it.

    D. Before I turned in my report, I written several different versions of it.

Identify and correctly use past, present, future, progressive, and perfect verb tenses.

13. Which sentence uses future perfect verb tense correctly?

    A. By the time I finish my shift tonight, I will have worked 13 straight hours.

    B. By the time I finish my shift tonight, I have worked 13 straight hours.

    C. By the time I finish my shift tonight, I had worked 13 straight hours.

    D. By the time I finish my shift tonight, I worked 13 straight hours.

Answers begin on page 105.

Follow Capitalization and Spelling Rules

Vocabulary

- capitalization
- italics
- quotation marks
- misspelled

Learning Goals

In this lesson, you will learn how to follow some capitalization and spelling rules. This includes learning how and when to use capital letters. You will also learn how to use italics and quotation marks with the titles of works. Finally, you will learn how to recognize and spell some commonly misspelled words.

Learn the Skill

Capitalization and spelling rules make it easier for people to read and understand text. Without capital letters, it would not be so easy to know the meaning of a word such as *jack*. The writer could mean either a person or a tool to help fix a flat tire. Capital letters at the beginning of sentences help us read more quickly. Along with periods, they help us know where one thought ends and another begins.

Italics and quotation marks also help us understand at a glance whether we're reading about Tom Sawyer the character or *Tom Sawyer* the novel.

Example 1

Capitalize Correctly

Using proper capitalization can help you communicate more clearly and professionally in school and at work. Below is a table that gives examples of what to capitalize and what not to capitalize.

Category	Capitalize	Do Not Capitalize
Personal names	Robert, Mrs. Smith, Uncle Jim	my mother, your uncle
Personal titles	Principal Smith, Governor Jones, Pope John Paul II	the principal, the governor, the pope
Ethnic/religious groups	Asian, Hispanic, African American, Muslim, Christian	Spanish citizens, religious
Holidays and special days	Ramadan, Memorial Day, Halloween	my birthday, a national holiday
Days, months, seasons	April, Wednesday	weekend, winter, summer
Brand names	Pepsi, Kleenex, Google, Ford Focus	cola, facial tissue, search engine, car
Buildings and monuments	Detroit Institute of Arts, Statue of Liberty, Holy Trinity Cathedral	the art museum, the memorial, the cathedral
Geographical terms	United States, Africa, Ohio River, Lake Erie, West Virginia, Pacific Northwest	southern Florida, the river in Ohio, the big lake, east, west, northern China

Note that personal titles are capitalized when directly followed by the person's name. For example: *President Donald Trump*, *General George Patton*, *Chief of Police Alesha Smith*. Otherwise, the title is not capitalized, even when it refers to a specific person. For example, *Gretchen Whitmer, the governor of Michigan, is a Democrat. Mrs. Smith is the chief of police of Centerville.*

Example 2

Write Titles of Works

Just as there are many rules for how to capitalize certain words, there are many rules for how to present the titles of works. Works include novels, short stories, poems, reports, articles, plays, and songs. They also include magazines, websites, newspapers, and journals. Italics and quotation marks are often used with the names of works.

Workplace Connection

At work, you might need to provide titles for reports, presentations, or memos. It would be helpful to know the basics of "headline-style" capitalization for these titles. Different organizations follow different guidelines. These are some of the basics:

- Capitalize the first and last words.

- Capitalize all other major words (nouns, verbs, adjectives, adverbs).

- Lowercase *the*, *a*, and *an*.

- Lowercase *and*, *but*, *for*, *or*, and *nor*.

- Lowercase prepositions. (Some guidelines say to capitalize prepositions that contain four or more letters.)

Think

Books often contain a preface, a forward, an index, or a glossary. These sections are often labeled in a book's table of contents. However, these words should get no special treatment when you write them. Do not use italics or quotation marks. For example: "The preface and glossary add 18 pages to the book!"

Use **italics** for the titles of books and the names of newspapers and magazines. For example:

- My favorite novel is *Huckleberry Finn* by Mark Twain.
- I just read an interesting newspaper article in *The Washington Post*.
- *Popular Mechanics* is my favorite magazine.

Use **quotation marks** for the titles of articles, essays, short stories, and chapters in books. For example:

- I read a great magazine article yesterday titled "Why You Should Have Dinner with Your Neighbors."
- The first chapter of *Huckleberry Finn* is titled "I Discover Moses and the Bulrushers."
- Stephen King wrote a short story called "The Lawnmower Man."

Example 3

Spell Correctly

Learning how to spell correctly involves a lot of practice and memorization. With English there is not always an obvious connection between how a word sounds and how it is spelled. However, certain guidelines can help you spell many types of words. Several of these guidelines are explained below.

Plurals

The most common way to make a singular noun plural is to add an *s* to the end of the word. For example: *manager – managers*

1. With words ending in *y*, you can usually follow these rules:

    a. If a consonant is directly before the *y*, change the *y* to *i* and add *es*. For example: library – libraries

    Remember: Consonants are all the letters that are not vowels. The vowels are *a, e, i, o,* and *u*.

    b. If a vowel is directly before the *y*, add *s*. For example: day – days

2. With words ending in *sh, ch, x, z, s,* or *ss*, add *es*. With words ending in *ze*, add *s*. For example: lunch – lunches, fox – foxes, size – sizes

3. For most words ending in *f* or *fe*, change the *f* or *fe* to *v* and add *es*. For example: wolf – wolves

    Some words don't fit this rule. For example: chief – chiefs

    The final sounds of plural words can give you a clue to their spellings. *Chiefs* has a /fs/ sound at the end. *Wolves* has a /vz/ sound. So if you hear /fs/, spell the plural with *fs* or *fes*. If you hear /vz/, spell the plural with *ves*.

4. Irregular plurals don't follow any of these rules. You have to memorize these spellings. For example: *man – men, child – children*

Patterns

1. Sometimes it is hard to remember whether a word ends in *le* or *el*. Remember that the *le* ending is much more common. Try to memorize the most common words with *el* endings. Then use *le* for the rest. Here are some of the most common words with *el* endings:

   level, model, travel, novel, channel, personnel, counsel, label, angel, tunnel, barrel, gospel, vessel, chapel, towel, rebel, gravel, diesel, cancel, marvel, shovel, jewel, nickel, parcel, unravel, caramel, flannel, funnel, bowel, quarrel, enamel

2. The long *a* sound is often spelled with *a* + consonant + *e* (as in *cake*). The patterns *ai* and *ay* (as in *rain* and *spray*) are also commonly used for the long *a* sound.

3. The long *i* sound is often spelled with *ight* (*bright*), *ie* (*pie*), *y* (*fly*), and *i* + consonant + *e* (*bite*).

Commonly Misspelled Words

Sometimes you just need to memorize spellings. When in doubt, check a dictionary.

Here are some commonly **misspelled** words:

a lot	grammar	pronunciation
accommodate	independent	publicly
appearance	maintenance	receive
believe	memento	rhythm
conscience	minuscule	separate
conscious	misspell	tomorrow
consensus	necessary	weird
definitely	occasion	which
embarrass	occurred	
government	privilege	

Test Tip

Carefully check the spellings of words with prefixes and suffixes. When the prefix *un* is followed by a base word that starts with the letter *n*, the word will have two *n*'s. For example: *unnatural, unnecessary, unneeded.* The same holds true for words that begin with *ir*. For example: *irregular, irresponsible, irrelevant.*

Check for Errors

In addition to using a dictionary to check for spelling errors, you can also use computer programs for writing, such as Microsoft Word. These programs often highlight possible spelling errors. But be careful. Not all of the suggested corrections are accurate, and some errors do not get highlighted.

Don't Forget

In addition to commonly misspelled words, you should also be mindful of commonly confused words. You learned about these in Lesson 1. They include *affect | effect*, *accept | except*, and *than | then*.

Guided Practice

Read this paragraph. Make corrections where needed. Then write the reason for each correction. Look for errors involving capitalization, formatting in titles, and spelling.

1. (1) Our teacher asked us to read the novel "War and Peace." (2) I said I thought that novel was definately too long. (3) "Well," said Ms. Lee, "you will have to discuss that with principal Jones." (4) I said I would prefer not to talk with the Principal. (5) I realized I should not have complained publically. (6) Next time I hope we read the poem *Nothing Gold Can Stay* by Robert Frost.

    1. _____

    2. _____

    3. _____

    4. _____

    5. _____

    6. _____

Answers: (1) *War and Peace.*—titles of novels should be italicized (2) **definitely**—*definately* is a misspelling (3) **Principal**—capitalize because it directly precedes the principal's name (4) **principal**—this should not be capitalized because it is not followed by the principal's name (5) **publicly**—*publically* is a misspelling (6) **"Nothing Gold Can Stay"**—poems should be in quotation marks, not italicized

Independent Practice

Choose the sentences that show correct use of capitalization and spelling.

2. Which sentence uses correct capitalization?
   A. Our town re-elected Mayor James in November.
   B. Our town re-elected Mayor James last Fall.
   C. The mayor of our town, Pat James, is my Uncle.
   D. Our Mayor was elected in November.

3. Which sentence presents titles of works correctly?
   A. She wrote the article *The NBA's Greatest Team.*
   B. She wrote the article "The NBA's Greatest Team."
   C. She used to work for *The Japan Times* newspaper.
   D. She used to work for "*The Japan Times*" newspaper.

4. Which sentence has every word spelled correctly?
   A. That company specialises in taxes.
   B. That company specializes in taxess.
   C. We have to finish our taxses before April 15.
   D. We have to finish our taxes before April 15.

5. Which sentence uses correct capitalization?
   A. Memorial Day is on the last Monday of May.
   B. Memorial day is on the last Monday of May.
   C. Memorial Day is on the last monday of May.
   D. Memorial Day is on the last Monday of may.

6. Which sentence uses italics and quotation marks correctly?
   A. "A Prayer for Owen Meany" is a novel by John Irving.
   B. A Prayer for Owen Meany is a novel by John Irving.
   C. *A Prayer for Owen Meany* is a novel by John Irving.
   D. A Prayer for Owen Meany is a novel by *John Irving*.

7. Which sentence has every word spelled correctly?
   A. I put shingels on three roofs last week.
   B. I put shingles on three rooves last week.
   C. I put shingels on three rooves last week.
   D. I put shingles on three roofs last week.

Lesson Review

In this lesson, you learned to

- demonstrate and identify the correct use of capitalization;
- demonstrate and identify the correct use of formatting in titles of works;
- use knowledge of word structure and origins, spelling patterns, and generalizations to correctly spell words.

Identify the correct use of capitalization.

8. Which sentence uses capitalization correctly?

   A. When I lived in Eastern Saudi Arabia, I celebrated an Islamic holiday called Eid.

   B. When I lived in eastern Saudi Arabia, I celebrated an Islamic holiday called Eid.

   C. When I lived in eastern Saudi arabia, I celebrated an Islamic holiday called Eid.

   D. When I lived in eastern Saudi Arabia, I celebrated an Islamic holiday called eid.

9. Read the sentence.

   I work for a company that fixes apple iPhones and other kinds of cell phones.

   Which word or words should be capitalized in this sentence?

   A. Apple

   B. Apple, Cell Phones

   C. Company, Apple

   D. Company

Identify the correct use of formatting in titles of works.

10. Read the sentences below. Choose the two sentences that have correct formatting of titles.

    A. The *Chicago Tribune* newspaper recently published a book review of *Where the Crawdads Sing* by Delia Owens.

    B. "Sports Illustrated" magazine recently published an article titled "Anthony Davis Trade Shakes Up the NBA."

    C. *Leaves of Grass* is a book of poems written by Walt Whitman. My favorite poem in the book is "Song of Myself."

    D. The Old Man and the Sea, a story by Ernest Hemingway, won the *Pulitzer Prize* in 1952.

    E. Helen Gurley Brown became chief editor of Cosmopolitan magazine in 1965.

Use knowledge of word structure and origins, spelling patterns, and generalizations to correctly spell words.

11. Read the sentence.

    The employees had several different beliefs about how the company should handle its bad publicity.

    Choose the <u>best</u> explanation of this sentence.

    A. All the words are spelled correctly. *Beliefs* is spelled the way it is because it ends in a /fs/ sound.

    B. *Beliefs* is spelled incorrectly. It should be *believes* because it ends in a /vz/ sound.

    C. *Handle* is spelled incorrectly. It should be *handel*.

    D. *Handle* is spelled correctly, with a silent *H*.

Answers begin on page 105.

Use Correct Punctuation: Commas

Learning Goals

In this lesson, you will learn to use commas in your writing. Commas help make the meaning clear in your writing. You will learn to use commas to join ideas in a sentence. You will learn how to use commas to separate items in a series. Also, you will learn how commas set off special words and phrases in sentences and in direct quotations.

Learn the Skill

Using commas in your writing will help readers better understand your meaning. Commas can link ideas in compound sentences. Commas are also used to separate lists of three or more items. They signal the reader to pause briefly when there are introductory words in a sentence. Commas also separate the words in a direct quotation from its source.

Example 1

Commas Separate Compound Sentences

Writers often combine short sentences into a compound sentence. A **compound sentence** has two or more **independent clauses** joined by a **coordinating conjunction**. Place a comma before the conjunction to show that another complete thought is coming in the sentence.

Read the following compound sentence. Notice the two independent clauses and the coordinating conjunction:

> I would have picked up milk at the store, but you didn't tell me that we needed it.

The independent clauses are *I would have picked up milk at the store* and *you didn't tell me that we needed it.* The coordinating conjunction *but* tells the reader that the two thoughts are connected. The comma before the conjunction gives the reader a pause before the second idea in the sentence.

Vocabulary

- compound sentence
- independent clause
- coordinating conjunction
- direct quotation

Check for Errors

Commas are the most-often used punctuation mark, but some writers make the mistake of using a comma whenever the word *and* is used. Be sure that your sentence has two complete thoughts before you separate them with *and*.

Example 2

Commas Separate Items in a Series

A list of three or more items is called a series. In a sentence, use commas to separate the items in a series. Placing a comma before the conjunction in a list will help avoid misunderstanding. Compare the following sentences:

> Tom went to the store to buy chicken, broccoli, carrots, macaroni and cheese.
> Tom went to the store to buy chicken, broccoli, carrots, macaroni, and cheese.

In the first sentence it is not clear if Tom is buying four items or five. Your reader might think that he is picking up a box of macaroni and cheese mix for dinner. But the comma before *and* in the second sentence makes it clear to the reader that Tom bought five separate items.

Example 3

Commas Set Off Words and Phrases

When you write a sentence that begins with a long phrase or clause as an introduction, a comma sets that introduction off from the rest of the sentence. Here are two examples of sentences with introductory phrases:

> When the rain began coming down in buckets, we decided to go inside.
> On the bench under the blooming magnolia tree, I waited for the bus.

Each of these sentences begins with information that adds detail to the main idea but is not necessary to the overall meaning of the sentence. The comma separates the beginning words from the main idea of the sentence. It makes the sentence easier to understand. Consider the following sentences:

> We decided to go inside when the rain began coming down in buckets.
> I waited for the bus on the bench under the blooming magnolia tree.

The comma is no longer needed when the same words are placed at the end of each sentence. Use commas to set off introductory words and phrases in your sentences.

Example 4

Commas Set Off Direct Addresses

Commas are used to set off special words that express conversation. Use a comma to set off words when:

- a person is directly addressed
- the first word of a sentence is yes or no
- a sentence ends with question words

Look at the following sentences and notice the commas.

> Mario, what time will the orchestra performance begin?
> No, I haven't found my keys.
> You heard that strange noise, didn't you?

These are examples of commas used in direct address.

Now read the following sentences. Notice there are no commas needed.

> Mario told us what time the orchestra performance will begin.
> No keys were found.
> Did you hear that strange noise?

In these sentences, no one is being addressed directly. No comma is needed.

Example 5

Commas Set Off Direct Quotations

In your writing, if you are repeating someone's exact words, that is called a **direct quotation**. Use quotation marks to show the words that were spoken. Place a comma between the speaker and the speaker's words.

Notice the placement of the quotation marks and the commas in the following sentences:

> Sara said, "My favorite restaurant is closed on Monday."
> "My favorite restaurant is closed on Mondays," said Sara.

In the first sentence, the speaker is named first, and her words follow. A comma is placed after the word *said* to separate the speaker from the quote.

In the second sentence, the quote comes first, followed by a comma that is inside the quotation marks. The comma separates the quote from the speaker.

When quoting a written work, the same rule applies for using commas. Look at the sentences below.

"This guide includes trails for all skill levels, from beginner to expert," stated the hiking guidebook.

The sign in the restroom at the gas station says, "All employees must wash their hands before returning to work."

Think

When you are writing conversation and are not sure where to put the comma, think about what the comma is doing in the sentence. If it separates the name of the speaker from the quote, then it does not belong inside the quotation marks. If the exact words come first in the sentence, put the comma inside the quotation marks, before the speaker.

Guided Practice

Read the paragraph and add commas where they are needed. Then write the reason to use each comma.

1. When I woke up on Tuesday morning I was excited. (2) My car was packed with my suitcase a cooler my towel and beach umbrella. I was going to the beach! (3) I had made plans with my friend to go on this trip but she broke her foot the day before. (4) "I'm sorry that you have to stay home and miss the waves" I told her. (5) She waved goodbye to me instead.

   _____

   _____

   _____

   _____

   Answers: Place comma after (1) **morning**—comma sets off the long introductory phrase from the main subject of the sentence (2) **suitcase, cooler, towel**—items in a series (3) **trip**—before the coordinating conjunction in a compound sentence (4) **waves** (inside the quotation mark)—separating a quote from the speaker (5) none

Independent Practice

Choose the sentence that shows a correct use of commas.

2. No the bus does not stop here anymore.
   A. No the bus does not, stop here anymore.
   B. No the bus, does not stop, here anymore.
   C. No, the bus does not stop here anymore.
   D. No the bus does not stop here, anymore.

3. After you get off the phone we can go to the mall.
   A. After you get off the phone, we can go to the mall.
   B. After you get off, the phone we can go to the mall.
   C. After you, get off the phone, we can go to the mall.
   D. After, you get off the phone we can go to the mall.

4. You will find parsley basil and oregano in the pantry.
   A. You will find parsley basil, and oregano in the pantry.
   B. You, will find parsley, basil, and oregano in the pantry.
   C. You will find parsley, basil, and oregano in the pantry.
   D. You will find parsley, basil, and oregano, in the pantry.

5. Though the movie starts at 7 we should arrive earlier for good seats.
   A. Though the movie starts at 7, we should arrive earlier for good seats.
   B. Though the movie starts, at 7 we should arrive earlier for good seats.
   C. Though the movie starts at 7 we should arrive, earlier, for good seats.
   D. Though, the movie starts at 7, we should arrive earlier for good seats.

6. Maria asked "What time do you think the movie will end?"
   A. Maria asked "What time, do you think the movie will end?"
   B. Maria asked, "What time do you think the movie will end?"
   C. Maria asked "What time do you think the movie will end?"
   D. Maria, asked "What time do you think the movie will end?"

7. Which sentence needs a comma?
   A. The mayor held a meeting with the town council members.
   B. They held the meeting but many of the members were absent.
   C. One topic they discussed was building a new town park.
   D. The new park would be in the center of town.

Lesson Review

In this lesson, you learned to

- use commas to separate independent clauses and items in a series;
- use commas to set off introductory words, direct address, yes or no, and question words in a sentence;
- use commas with quotation marks to separate exact speech from the speaker.

Use commas to separate independent clauses and items in a series.

8. Which sentence uses a comma correctly?

   A. His birthday is Saturday and he wants, a party.

   B. I wanted to get a cat, but my landlord won't allow it.

   C. The lights the sounds and the crowds are things I love about the city.

   D. The first thing, I noticed about the car was that the paint was peeling.

9. Read the sentence.

   Would you like to have tacos, burritos or fajitas for dinner tonight?

   Where should a comma be placed in this sentence?

   A. after the word *burritos*

   B. after the word *you*

   C. after the word *dinner*

   D. after the word *fajitas*

Use commas to set off introductory words, direct address, yes or no, and question words in a sentence.

10. Read the sentences below. Choose the three sentences that use commas correctly.

    A. Yes, the furniture is going to be delivered, on Saturday.

    B. Because we were not sure of the address, we did not find the house.

    C. She is still going to deliver the package to your cousin, right?

    D. Pablo, I think you should mow the lawn today.

11. Which sentence uses a comma correctly?

    A. Yes, the movers will be here on Tuesday.

    B. I'm sorry for, the delay in calling you back.

    C. The books are ready for pickup, at the library.

    D. We were unhappy and the company offered to help us.

Use commas with quotation marks to separate exact words from the speaker

12. Read the sentence.

    We will meet you at the bank to sign the papers said Marcia.

    Which sentence shows the correct placement of the quotation marks and commas?

    A. "We will meet you at the bank to sign the papers" said Marcia.

    B. "We will meet you at the bank to sign the papers" said, Marcia.

    C. "We will meet you at the bank to sign the papers", said Marcia.

    D. "We will meet you at the bank to sign the papers," said Marcia.

Answers begin on page 106.

Use a Variety of Sentence Styles

Learning Goals

In this lesson, you will learn how language changes when writing, speaking, reading, or listening. You will learn how to change the length of a sentence to give it a different meaning. You will also learn what dialects and registers are and how they are used in texts.

Learn the Skill

Sentences come in many different forms. The way a sentence is written can change its meaning. We often change the way we use language depending on the setting and the audience. For example, the way we write is often different from the way we speak. The way we speak to a boss is usually different from the way we speak to a friend. Also, in different places, people use different dialects or registers when writing and speaking.

Example 1

Changing Language for Different Uses

People tend to use language a little differently depending on whether they are writing, speaking, reading, or listening. Compare these two sentences. Think about how and where each would be used:

> See you tomorrow morning at 9!
> I will see you tomorrow at 9:00 am.

Both sentences express the same idea. The first sentence is more conversational and more likely to be used when speaking. It's shorter, but in person it would be clear who the *you* is in the sentence. The second sentence is longer and includes more precise details. It is more likely to be used in writing. It would also sound more formal out loud.

In language, everything depends on context. For example, the second sentence might fit when spoken in a formal conversation, such as when scheduling a job interview or an appointment. Also, certain types of writing work better with informal language. Consider the following sentence:

> See ya tomorrow @ 9

Texting and quick notes are forms of writing that require less formal language because of their fast and short nature. They tend to be less formal than writing a letter or email because they are sent to friends and family rather than teachers and coworkers.

Vocabulary

- dialect
- register
- abbreviation
- contraction
- slang

Real-World Connection

Think about how you naturally communicate out loud and in writing. What comes naturally to you?

Don't Forget

In Lesson 2, you learned about prepositions and prepositional phrases. They can give more information about things. Remember that some common prepositions are: *of, in to, into, for, with, on, at, from, by, between, before, after, below,* and *about.* A prepositional phrase begins with a preposition and ends with the object of that preposition (for example: *at home* or *with you*). You can use prepositions to add details and lengthen sentences.

Don't Forget

In Lesson 2, you learned about conjunctions. Remember that some common conjunctions are: *and, but, or, not, yet, so, for, because, although, if,* and *since.* In most cases, you will need a conjunction to combine sentences.

Example 2

Changing Sentence Length for Meaning

A good writer uses varying sentence lengths to create different meanings. This also helps keep the reader engaged. There are a few ways you can change sentence length to create an effect: lengthen, shorten, or combine.

Lengthening a sentence can help you add details and make it more interesting to your reader. Consider the following sentence:

> The girl rode her bicycle to work.

This sentence states a clear idea, but adding more detail can give it context and help create a more interesting story. To make it longer, you could ask yourself *how* or *why* the subject in your sentence is doing what she's doing. For example:

> The girl pedaled as quickly as she could on her bicycle to make it to work on time.

In this longer version of the sentence, the reader better understands how the girl was riding her bike and why.

On the other hand, shortening a long sentence can help make the sentence more clear or more powerful. Sometimes, too many long sentences can get in the way of meaning. Consider the following sentences:

> Having been sick for quite some time, she still decided to get on stage and sing as best as she could.
> Despite being sick, she sang her heart out on stage.

The second sentence is clearer and focuses on the main points: that she was sick and that she still tried hard to sing well. By shortening the sentence and focusing on those two conflicting details, the second sentence has a more dramatic effect. Also, short sentences can be more effective when you need to get your point across quickly. For example, yelling *Over here!* will work a lot better to get a taxi driver's attention than: *I would like a ride home. Please pick me up over here!*

Finally, you can combine two sentences to change sentence lengths or create smoother writing. Consider the following statements:

> He likes to read. He likes to write. He likes to play the piano.
> He likes to read, write, and play the piano.

The combined sentence above includes all three things he likes to do, and it is less choppy than the three separate sentences. Combining sentences can also help make connections between ideas. For instance, the following sentences can combine to show that the rain in April is the reason why the speaker's garden is growing so well.

> It rained a lot this April. My garden is growing a lot of healthy vegetables.
> Since it rained a lot this April, my garden is growing a lot of healthy vegetables.

Example 3

Comparing Dialects and Registers

Within the English language, people in different regions use different terms to mean the same thing. A **dialect** is a way of speaking that is used in a particular area. It can include vocabulary and grammar. For example, someone in the southern U.S. might say *y'all* to address more than one person. Someone in the northern U.S. would likely say *you* or *you guys*. People in the North would understand someone saying *y'all*, but they probably wouldn't use it themselves.

Dialects are often used in literature to help show where a character is from or where a scene is taking place. Read the following paragraph from *The Adventures of Tom Sawyer* by Mark Twain. In this famous scene, Tom Sawyer is tricking his friend Ben into helping him paint a fence.

> "No—no—I <u>reckon</u> it wouldn't hardly do, Ben. You see, Aunt Polly's <u>awful</u> particular about this fence—right here on the street, you know— but if it was the back fence I wouldn't mind and SHE wouldn't. Yes, she's awful particular about this fence; <u>it's got to</u> be done very careful; I reckon there <u>ain't</u> one boy in a thousand, maybe two thousand, that can do it the way it's got to be done."

Review the underlined words and phrases. They are examples of Tom's specific dialect. It shows that he is speaking casually and that he is from a southern region.

Another way that language can vary is in **register**. Register is the level of formality in the language. As you learned in Example 1, your formality often needs to change depending on your audience and purpose. For example, your register would be more formal with a boss or stranger than with a friend or family member. Your register would be more formal in an academic or legal paper than in a blog post or friendly letter.

Formal language typically uses full words and correct grammar. Informal language may use **abbreviations**, **contractions**, **slang**, and improper grammar. Generally, formal language is less personal.

Workplace Connection

Many things can affect which register should be used when speaking or writing. If you are not sure, it is generally better to use a more formal tone in a professional or academic setting.

Read the following passage from *Peter Pan* by J. M. Barrie.

"What's your name?" he asked.

"Wendy Moira Angela Darling," she replied. "What is your name?"

"Peter Pan."

She asked where he lived.

"Second to the right," said Peter, "and then straight on till morning."

"What a funny address!"

"No, it isn't," he said.

"I mean," Wendy said nicely, remembering that she was hostess, "is that what they put on the letters?"

He wished she had not mentioned letters.

"Don't get any letters," he said.

"But your mother gets letters?"

"Don't have a mother," he said.

In this story, the writer uses more informal language for Peter than for Wendy. Peter speaks using incomplete sentences and contractions (*isn't* and *don't*). These help him appear young, casual, and relaxed. Those are all important parts of Peter Pan's personality. Meanwhile, Wendy seems more formal. She uses full words and longer sentences. The two registers help show how different the characters are.

Guided Practice

Read the paragraph. Assume the paragraph was written for a personal blog.

(1) My friend Eliza worked hard for a long time to write a play. (2) It premiered last weekend, so I went to see it at the theater. (3) It is a comedy, but at times, I found myself feeling sad for the main character, who suffered a terrible injury from a boating accident. (4) At the end, I heard everyone clap. Then I felt extremely proud of my friend.

1. Rewrite the paragraph above using any of the following sentence revision strategies: shorten, lengthen, combine. Then, explain the reasons for your revisions.

   _____

   _____

   _____

   _____

   _____

   _____

   _____

   _____

Think

Who is the audience? What is the purpose for communicating? How can the sentence style be changed in length, register, or other ways to create the effect you want?

Answer: There are many ways to revise this paragraph. Here is one example to make it more interesting to readers, while keeping it somewhat informal:

My friend Eliza worked passionately day and night to write a play. I went to see the premiere at the theater last weekend. Although it's a comedy, I often felt sad for the main character, who suffered a terrible injury in a boating accident. At the end, when I heard everyone clap, I felt extremely proud of my friend.

In this revision, the first sentence was lengthened to add interesting details. The second and third sentences were both shortened to add clarity and create a smoother reading experience. Finally, the last two sentences were combined for a more powerful effect.

Independent Practice

For questions 2–5, rewrite each sentence in a more formal style.

2. I'm not gonna make it tomorrow.

   _____

3. Annie got an expensive new purse.

   _____

4. What do you want for lunch today?

   _____

5. George made an appointment for next month.

   _____

6. Which sentence would most likely be used when speaking to a close friend?

   A. I don't believe I received your message.

   B. I'd love to come!

   C. I apologize for being late.

   D. Please let me know your availability for next week.

7. Read the sentences.

   > Tide pools can be as small as a few inches. Tide pools are home to a lot of sea creatures.

   Choose the two sentences that <u>best</u> combine the sentences above.

   A. Tide pools can be as small as a few inches, but they are home to a lot of sea creatures.

   B. Tide pools can be as small as a few inches, and tide pools are home to a lot of sea creatures.

   C. Although tide pools can be as small as a few inches, they are home to a lot of sea creatures.

   D. Since tide pools can be as small as a few inches, they are home to a lot of sea creatures.

8. Read the paragraph.

   (1) Maria works as a taxi driver, and weekends are the busiest times for her. (2) Last Friday, she picked up a mysterious man from the airport. (3) He was wearing sunglasses and a leather jacket, and he typed very quickly on his cell phone. (4) Given that Maria watches a lot of popular TV shows, she can recognize actors' faces and quickly realized that he was a famous comedian from one of her favorite shows!

   Which sentence should be shortened to be more impactful?

   A. 1

   B. 2

   C. 3

   D. 4

9. Which sentence shows an example of dialect?

   A. Thanks for all your help!

   B. He read his book until dawn.

   C. She's outside gardening.

   D. You betcha!

Lesson Review

In this lesson, you learned to

- change the length of a sentence for meaning, audience, and style;
- compare dialects and registers used in literary texts.

Modify the length of a sentence for meaning, audience, and style.

10. Read the sentence.

> Rick is gonna be out from July 1st through July 5th.

Which option shows the best way to lengthen the sentence to make it appropriate for a formal workplace?

A. Rick is going to be out from July 1st through July 5th.

B. Rick is gonna be out of the office from July 1st through July 5th.

C. From July 1st through July 5th, Rick will be out.

D. Rick will be out of the office from July 1st through July 5th.

11. Read the paragraph.

> The gravitational pull of the sun on the earth causes waves. The gravitational pull of the moon on the earth also causes waves. All of these waves are called tidal waves.

Which option below best combines the sentences above for clarity?

A. The gravitational pull of the sun on the earth causes tidal waves. The gravitational pull of the moon on the earth also causes tidal waves.

B. The gravitational pull of the sun and the moon on the earth causes tidal waves.

C. The gravitational pull of the sun and the gravitational pull of the moon on earth cause tidal waves.

D. The gravitational pull of the sun on the earth causes tidal waves, and so does the gravitational pull of the moon on the earth.

12. Read the sentence.

> Greta smelled the cherry pie, and right away, her memory shot back to a time when she used to spend afternoons baking with her grandmother.

Which option shows the best way to shorten the sentence to make it more powerful?

A. After smelling the cherry pie, right away, Greta's memory shot back to her and her grandmother spending afternoons baking.

B. Greta smelled the cherry pie, and right away, her memory shot back to her and her grandmother baking in the afternoons.

C. As soon as Greta smelled the cherry pie, her memory shot back to afternoons spent baking with her grandmother.

D. Right away, when Greta smelled the cherry pie, her memory shot back to afternoons spent baking with her grandmother.

13. Identify the two sentences below that would be appropriate when writing to a teacher.

    A. I'm gonna need some more time to finish the assignment.

    B. I would like to ask you some questions about the assignment.

    C. I don't really understand the assignment.

    D. I am almost finished with the assignment and will turn it in soon.

Compare dialects and registers used in literary texts.

14. Read the passage from *White Fang* by Jack London.

    Henry looked at him commiseratingly, and said, "I'll be almighty glad when this trip's over."

    "What d'ye mean by that?" Bill demanded.

    Which word or phrase from the passage is an example of dialect?

    A. I'll be

    B. trip's

    C. What d'ye

    D. commiseratingly

15. Read the passage from *The Enchanted Castle* by E. Nesbit.

    Dear Aunt,—

    I am afraid you will not see me again for some time. A lady in a motor-car has adopted me, and we are going straight to the coast and then in a ship. It is useless to try to follow me. Farewell, and may you be happy. I hope you enjoyed the fair.

    Mabel

    What type of language register is used in the passage?

    A. formal

    B. informal

    C. dialect

    D. letter

16. Identify the three types of language that might be used in an informal register.

    A. slang

    B. correct grammar

    C. full words

    D. abbreviations

    E. contractions

Test Tip

If you are not sure which sentence or sentences are best for a certain audience or register, try focusing on how they sound in your head. Other options may use correct grammar, but many times you can decide which option is best by how it sounds out loud. Does it flow naturally and clearly?

Answers begin on page 106.

Skill Check

Lesson 1

1. Read the sentence.

    Gene and I order pizza every Friday night.

    Which part of the sentence is the predicate?

    A. Gene and I

    B. and I order pizza

    C. order pizza

    D. order pizza every Friday night

2. Read the sentence.

    My friend has two tiny, Dalmatian, well-behaved, black and white puppies.

    Rewrite the sentence to put the adjectives in the correct order.

    _____

    _____

3. Which of the following sentences is written correctly?

    A. Patricia, who works at the coffee shop, is organizing the community farmers market.

    B. Patricia who works at the coffee shop is organizing the community farmers market.

    C. Patricia is organizing the farmers market, who works at the coffee shop.

    D. Patricia, who works at the coffee shop, and who is organizing the community farmers market.

4. Read the paragraph.

    Here are some tips for new drivers: Do not roll threw stop signs. To slow down to a stop, take your foot off the gas pedal and gently hit the break. Its important to make sure you keep your eyes on the road.

    Circle the words that are incorrect. Then, write the correct replacements.

    _____

    _____

Lesson 2

5. Which sentence uses a preposition?

    A. My flight was delayed, so I read my book.

    B. Well, I read my book.

    C. I read my book while waiting at the airport.

    D. My flight was delayed, but at least I had my book.

6. Which sentence uses a correlative conjunction correctly?

    A. We can order both pizza and sushi.

    B. We can order not only pizza and sushi.

    C. We can order both pizza or sushi.

    D. We can order either pizza and sushi.

7. Select the three sentences from the list below that use modal auxiliaries.

    A. I study for every test.

    B. I can study for the test after class.

    C. I might study for the test.

    D. Can you help me study for the test?

    E. I don't like studying for tests.

8. Which sentence uses a past participle correctly?

   A. She have seen that movie several times.

   B. She seen that movie several times.

   C. She has saw that movie several times.

   D. She has seen that movie several times.

9. Which sentence uses the present progressive verb tense correctly?

   A. I was working in my garden.

   B. I am working in my garden.

   C. I worked in my garden.

   D. I will work in my garden.

Lesson 3

10. Read the paragraph.

    My Birthday is in June. Every year, I take a weekend trip around that time. This year, my Sister and I will leave on a friday to drive to lake Michigan. I love going to the beach in the summer!

    Rewrite the paragraph to fix the capitalization errors.

    _____

    _____

    _____

    _____

11. Which sentence presents titles of works correctly?

    A. I read a fantastic article titled *How to be Happier* in "The New York Times."

    B. I read a fantastic article titled "How to be Happier" in *The New York Times*.

    C. I read a fantastic article titled How to be Happier in The New York Times.

    D. I read a fantastic article titled "How to be Happier" in "The New York Times."

12. Select the pair of words that shows the correct singular and plural versions.

    A. fox   foxs

    B. wolf   wolfs

    C. canary   canaries

    D. sheep   sheeps

13. Which sentence contains a spelling error?

    A. The lumberjack wore a flannel shirt and carried a shovel.

    B. The man drove slowly down the gravel road in the rain.

    C. The child was so well behaved they called her an angel.

    D. The remote control was broken, so we couldn't change the channle.

Lesson 4

14. Read the paragraph.

    Congress chose the District of Columbia to be the capital of the United States government in 1790. Congress first met in Washington, D.C., in 1800 although construction on the first phase of the Capitol was not done until 1826. Moving forward in time to today millions of people visit Washington, D.C., to see the Capitol the White House the Library of Congress and many other monuments.

    Insert commas in the correct places.

15. Which sentence uses a comma correctly?

    A. When I first saw the new community garden, I was stunned.

    B. I was stunned, when I first saw the community garden.

    C. After, the first day of class I felt a lot less nervous.

    D. I felt a lot less nervous, after the first day of class.

16. Which sentence uses a comma correctly?

    A. Grace are you, coming over for dinner?

    B. Yes she does.

    C. You haven't seen my wallet, have you?

    D. I'm over here Eric!

17. Which sentence uses a comma correctly?

    A. Aida said, "I think we should leave for the party in an hour."

    B. Aida, said "I think we should leave for the party in an hour."

    C. "I think we should leave for the party in an hour" Aida said.

    D. "I think, we should leave for the party in an hour" Aida said.

Lesson 5

18. Read the sentence.

    The movie had just started, and then I spilled my popcorn, which went all over the floor.

    Which new sentence shows the best way to shorten the sentence above?

    A. The movie had just started, and then I spilled my popcorn all over the floor.

    B. The movie had just started when I spilled my popcorn all over the floor.

    C. The movie had just started when I spilled my popcorn, which went all over the floor.

    D. When the movie had just started, I spilled my popcorn, which went all over the floor.

19. Read the sentences.

    In the winter, I like to sit by the fireplace. I like to drink hot chocolate. Finally, I like to read a good book.

    Write a new sentence that combines all three sentences above.

    _____

    _____

    _____

20. What is the correct definition of dialect?

    A. the level of formality in language

    B. a shortened word formed by combining two words and replacing letters with an apostrophe

    C. a way of speaking that is particular to a specific area

    D. a shortened form of a word or phrase that often ends with a period

21. Which sentence uses formal language?

    A. That conference Sophia went to was last weekend.

    B. Sophia went to the conference with a bunch of students.

    C. Sophia didn't want to attend the conference without her students.

    D. Sophia attended the leadership conference with thirteen of her students.

Answers begin on page 107.

UNIT 2

Vocabulary

This unit will cover the following topics:

- Determining definitions
- Using topic words
- Using relationship words

Sid has been a heavy equipment operator for Smith County for about 12 years. He has learned that safety is very important when working with heavy machinery. Recently, Sid has been asked to operate a new crane. He wants to learn as much as possible about using the machine safely.

When Sid started to read the training manual for the crane, he found some words he did not understand. Because he studied vocabulary in his adult education course, he was able to better determine the definitions of the unknown words by looking for context clues and noticing prefixes and suffixes. He was also able to use the dictionary to understand some of the harder words.

Using context clues, identifying root words and their prefixes and suffixes, and learning to use the dictionary are all important steps in being able to understand instructions and directions better. In Sid's case, these skills helped to keep him and his co-workers safe.

Determine Definitions

Vocabulary

- context clues
- root
- affix
- reference material

Learning Goals

In this lesson, you will learn what to do when you come across words you don't know while reading. You will learn about context clues, Greek and Latin roots and affixes, and reference materials. Learning how to use these tools will help you understand words you don't know.

Learn the Skill

There is no single best way to determine the definition of a new word while reading. Different methods work in different situations. It is best to have several from which to choose.

When you see a new word, you must decide how important it is. You must also consider how much time you have to spend figuring it out. If a new word seems unimportant to the central meaning of a reading, you might want to use context, or the words around the new word, to guess at its meaning. This will allow you to continue reading with just a short pause.

If a word seems to be important, however, you might want to take some time to learn about it. See if your knowledge of word parts can help you understand the word. If that doesn't work, then take the time to learn about the word in a dictionary.

Example 1

Context Clues

Readers can often figure out the meanings of new words by using **context clues**. This involves using the words or sentences before and after the new word to help you understand that word. Comparisons, contrasts, explanations, and examples are four types of context clues.

Here is an example of a context clue that uses contrast. Two things are being compared to show how they are different. Can you guess the meaning of the underlined word?

Lou used to be <u>*vocal*</u>*, but now he rarely speaks.*

In this sentence, the word *but* tells you that some things are being contrasted. On one side of *but* is the word *vocal*. On the other side is the term *rarely speaks*. You can guess that *vocal* is probably the opposite of *rarely speaks*. So, you were right if you guessed that *vocal* is used to describe someone who talks a lot.

Here is an example of a context clue that uses comparison:

Lou has become so <u>*vocal*</u>*. He can't keep his mouth shut!*

This context clue shows how two things are alike. Readers who don't know the meaning of *vocal* can guess that it is like not being able to keep one's mouth shut.

Here is an example of a context clue that uses an explanation:

Lou is so <u>*vocal*</u>*. I'm becoming tired of his non-stop talking.*

Here, *his non-stop talking* is used as an explanation for how Lou is *vocal*.

Here is an example of a context clue that gives an example:

Lou is so <u>*vocal*</u>*. He talked non-stop on the bus yesterday for 90 minutes!*

Here, readers can guess the meaning of *vocal* based on the example of his actions. If he talked non-stop for 90 minutes, you can guess that *vocal* describes someone who talks a lot.

Workplace Connection

Context clues come in many forms. They are not always written or spoken. Look around your environment for context clues. These may be in the form of images, sounds, or even smells. Learn to use all of the context clues around you.

Think

Knowledge of roots and suffixes can be very helpful. But roots and suffixes can also be misleading. Word meanings change over time, and a word used today may not mean something close to its root meaning. For example, most people won't be helped in understanding the common meaning of the word *calorie* by knowing that its Latin root means "heat."

Example 2

Greek and Latin roots and affixes

Many English words have roots or affixes that came from Greek or Latin. A **root** is the most basic part of a word. **Affixes** are word parts at the beginning or end of a root that create a new word with a new meaning. Prefixes are added to the beginning. Suffixes are added to the end.

This word has a Latin root, a prefix, and a suffix:

sympathetic

The root is *path*. It means "feeling or suffering" in Greek. Think of the word *pathetic*, which often involves feelings of sadness or suffering.

The prefix is *sym-*. It means "together" or "with." Think of the word *symphony*, which involves people playing music together.

The suffix is *-ic*. It means "nature of" or "like." Think of the word *metallic*, which describes something that has the nature of, or is like, metal.

If you know the meanings of common roots and affixes, you can more easily figure out the meanings of many words you don't know.

Examples:

Roots	Prefixes	Suffixes
bio (life)	*aqua-* (water)	*-able*, *-ible* (able, capable)
geo (earth, ground)	*auto-* (self)	*-en* (made of, to make)
graph (write)	*bi-* (two)	*-er* (one who)
man (hand)	*pre-* (before)	*-ic* (nature of, like)
nov (new)	*re-* (again)	*-logy* (study or science of)
therm (heat)	*tele-* (far, distant)	*-some* (like, tending to)

Example 3

Reference materials

Sometimes, context and knowledge of roots and suffixes will not give you the full meaning of a word. Other times, you will want to make sure you really understand the meaning. In such cases, use **reference materials**.

The first place you might want to look is a dictionary. This will tell you the meaning(s) of a word. It will also show you how the word is pronounced and used in a sentence. There are many good dictionaries online and in print.

A thesaurus is another good resource. It will provide synonyms, which are words that are like the one you are trying to define. It will also provide antonyms, which are words that are opposite, or nearly opposite, the one you are trying to define.

Sample Dictionary Entry:

essential (adjective) *i-sen(t)-shul*
1. very important and necessary; required
2. very basic

Sample Thesaurus Entry:

essential (adj.)
meaning: important, vital
Synonyms: crucial, fundamental, imperative, main, necessary, needed
Antonyms: inessential, minor, needless, nonessential, optional, secondary, trivial, unimportant, unnecessary

Test Tip

Building your vocabulary is essential to doing well on the TABE test. While it is important to learn some ways to determine definitions, it is also important to remember new words. Regularly reading challenging material is a good way to develop your vocabulary.

Guided Practice

Read the sentence below. Then correct the statements that follow. Write the reason for each correction.

> It was cold outside, so I wore my thermal socks, which are designed to keep feet warm.

1. In the word *thermal*, *therm-* is a suffix and *-al* is a prefix.

2. In this sentence, a contrast-type context clue helps readers determine the meaning of *thermal socks*.

3. The context tells readers that *thermal* is probably related to the word *wet*.

4. Readers can look in a dictionary to find a synonym for *thermal*.

Answers: (1) *Therm* is the root, and *-al* is the suffix. (2) An **explanation-type** context clue helps readers determine the meaning. (3) The context tells readers that *thermal* is probably related to the word **heat**. (4) Readers can look in a **thesaurus** to find a synonym for *thermal*.

Independent Practice

Choose the sentences that show the best understanding of determining definitions.

2. Which sentence correctly describes the word *biography*?

   A. *Biography* contains the root words *bio* and *graph*.

   B. *Biography* contains the root word *graph* and the prefix *bio-*.

   C. *Biography* contains the root word *graph* and the suffix *bio-*.

   D. *Biography* contains the root word *bio* and the suffix *-graphy*.

3. Which sentence has an example-type context clue for the word *biography*?

   A. A biography is a nonfiction book about a person that's written by another person.

   B. Biographies and autobiographies both tell the story of a person's life.

   C. My favorite biography is *The Fiery Trial: Abraham Lincoln and American Slavery*.

   D. Unlike biographies, autobiographies are written by the subject of the book.

4. If you want to know which other words have similar meanings to the word *ugly*, which kind of resource should you use?

   A. a science book

   B. a dictionary

   C. a thesaurus

   D. an atlas

Use context clues to determine the meaning of the underlined word below.

A well-known <u>aphorism</u> is, "A jack of all trades is master of none."

5. What is the most likely definition of *aphorism*?

   A. a word that few people understand

   B. a saying that has a general truth

   C. a job that does not pay well

   D. a person who has many talents

6. Which type of context clue appears in question 5?

   A. explanation

   B. comparison

   C. contrast

   D. example

Think

Synonyms are similar to each other. This does not mean they are the same. Words with similar meanings often have different connotations. These are the ideas or feelings associated with each word. For example, *childish* and *youthful* are synonyms. But *childish* has a negative connotation while *youthful* does not.

Lesson Review

In this lesson, you learned to determine definitions by using

- context clues,
- reference materials, and
- affixes and roots.

7. Which word below means "worked by hand"? Use the roots and suffixes you learned about earlier in this lesson.

   A. grapheme

   B. vivacious

   C. novel

   D. manual

8. Read the sentences.

   > Vultures are scavenging birds of prey. They rarely attack live animals. Instead, they eat carrion.

   Based on context clues, which word likely means "dead or decaying flesh"?

   A. scavenging

   B. vibrant

   C. carrion

   D. toxins

Read the thesaurus entry and example sentence below.

censure (verb)
meaning: condemn; criticize severely
Synonyms: admonish, berate, chastise, denounce, rebuke, reprimand, scold
Antonyms: approve, commend, compliment, flatter, forgive, praise, defend, endorse

Example: The judge censured the lawyer for being dishonest.

9. Which sentence shows an example of the opposite meaning for the word *censure*?

   A. The judge commended the lawyer for being honest.

   B. The judge admonished the lawyer for being dishonest.

   C. The judge denounced the lawyer for being dishonest.

   D. The judge reprimanded the lawyer for being dishonest.

Use roots and suffixes, context clues, or reference material to determine the meaning of the underlined phrase.

10. Read the sentence.

    > The dock workers were from all over the world. In total, they spoke more than 20 languages. Aside from hand gestures, the only way they could communicate was with a common <u>lingua franca</u>: English.

    Choose the best meaning of the underlined phrase.

    A. the French language, which is commonly used for communication among dock workers

    B. a cellphone app that allows users to communicate with each other in English

    C. a language used for communication among people who speak different first languages

    D. a type of sign language used for communication among people who speak different first languages

Answers begin on page 107.

Use Topic Words

Learning Goals

In this lesson, you will learn how topic words are used in writing about a specific subject. Understanding the meanings of topic words will help you understand the information you are reading. You will learn how an author's explanation, context clues, your knowledge of word parts, and a dictionary can help you find the meaning of a topic word.

Learn the Skill

Authors will use many words that are related to the specific subject they are writing about. For example, a book about cooking might use words like *blend*, *baste*, *poach*, and *blanch*. You must know the meanings of these words in order to understand the text. You can often figure out the meanings of topic words from the author's explanation, context clues, familiar word parts, or by using a dictionary.

Example 1

Use the Author's Explanation to Find the Meaning of Topic Words

Read the following sentences. Notice words the author uses to explain the process of braising to give the reader better understanding.

> One way to cook a tougher cut of meat is to braise it. When braising, first sear the meat in a hot pan until it turns brown, then gently simmer it in a small amount of liquid over low heat in a covered pan until tender.

From the author's description in this paragraph, you can tell that the process of braising involves browning meat in a pan and then cooking it slowly in liquid to make it tender. *Braise*, *sear*, and *simmer* are topic words related to cooking.

Vocabulary

- topic word

Think

What is the paragraph about? What words in the paragraph relate specifically to this topic?

© New Readers Press. All rights reserved.

Test Tip

Look for clues such as *like, unlike, similar,* or *opposite* to figure out the meaning of a topic word.

Think

Pay attention to words with similar endings or beginnings and ask yourself how they are related in the passage. Even if you come across a word you have never seen before, you may be able to understand its meaning from the related words.

Example 2

Use Context Clues to Understand Topic Words

The context of a word includes the other words around it that help explain its meaning. Read the following passage and look for words that give clues to the meaning of the topic words.

> Houses built by the ancient Aztecs had common characteristics. The walls were mainly built from adobe bricks, and many houses had peaked straw roofs. In the big city of Tenochtitlán, the houses were often smaller than those in the rural areas.

This paragraph is about the houses built by ancient Aztec people. Topic words that you should have noticed include *Aztecs, adobe,* and *Tenochtitlán*.

Example 3

Use Knowledge of Word Parts to Find the Meaning of Topic Words

You may read a passage that has topic words that begin or end with the same word part. Knowing the meaning of some suffixes and prefixes can help you understand how the words are related to the topic and to each other.

Look at the chart below. It shows some common word parts and their meanings:

Word Part	Meaning
-ology	the study of
-sphere	like a ball
auto-	self
astro-	star

Guided Practice

1. Read the paragraph below. Underline the topic words. How are all the words that end in *-sphere* related? How do they relate to the topic of meteorology?

   Meteorology is the study of the way changes in Earth's atmosphere cause weather. The atmosphere is made up of five main layers—the troposphere, the stratosphere, the mesosphere, the thermosphere, and the exosphere. All the weather on Earth forms in the troposphere.

   _____

   _____

   _____

   _____

   Answer: The topic words are *meteorology, atmosphere, troposphere, stratosphere, mesosphere, thermosphere,* and *exosphere*. The words that end in *-sphere* are all layers of the atmosphere that surrounds the earth. Meteorology is the study of the changes in the layers of the atmosphere.

Check for Errors

If the author's words, context, and word parts do not help you understand the meaning of a word, use a dictionary to find the definition. A dictionary will often provide a sample sentence using the word along with its meaning. You can check the sentence to get a better understanding of how to use the word.

Think

When you come across an unfamiliar word, look for clues in word parts, context, and related words in the passage. Also, notice how the word is used in the passage.

Independent Practice

For questions 2–6, underline the topic word(s) in each sentence.

2. The Renaissance was a time of great learning and scientific achievement in world history.

3. The theory of how Earth's crust is changing and moving is called continental drift or plate tectonics.

4. An aquarium that has a balanced ecosystem will provide a happy home for your fish.

5. The "airbag warning" light will flash when there is a problem with the supplemental restraint system in the vehicle.

6. Hieroglyphics carved into the wall of the pyramid showed the daily tasks of ancient Egyptian people.

Lesson Review

In this lesson, you learned to

- understand topic words from the author's explanation,
- understand topic words from context clues,
- use familiar word parts to understand the meaning of topic words.

Read the paragraph. Then answer questions 7–9.

Purchasing Car Insurance

If you want to own a car, you must buy an insurance <u>policy</u> that protects you if you have an accident. The <u>premium</u> that you will pay for your policy will be based on your age, your driving record, the amount of <u>coverage</u> that you want, and the size of the <u>deductible</u> that you would pay. A deductible is the amount you pay every time you file a claim. If you choose a higher deductible, the yearly premium will be lower than if you choose a smaller deductible.

Choose the sentences that show a correct use of grammar.

7. Which sentence uses the word *premium* correctly?

   A. How much premium do you have to pay when you file a claim?

   B. The premium on my policy went down because I am a safe driver.

   C. An insurance agent called me about purchasing a new premium.

   D. My deductible went down because I chose a lower premium.

8. Which sentence uses the word *policy* correctly?

   A. I make a car insurance policy every six months.

   B. We have a lower policy since we bought a new car.

   C. The policy that I paid was more than the cost of the repair.

   D. Our policy covers the three cars in our family.

9. Which sentence uses the word *deductible* correctly?

   A. She paid the $500 deductible, and the insurance company paid the rest of the repair costs after the accident.

   B. My deductible expires in June.

   C. How much of the deductible do you pay when you renew your policy?

   D. His deductible covers vehicle repairs and damage to property.

Answers begin on page 108.

Use Relationship Words

Vocabulary

- relationship words
- comparison
- contrast

Think

When you see a relationship word in a sentence, ask yourself what pieces of information it is connecting. Does it show contrast, likeness, cause, or effect? When you understand the relationship, you will better understand the meaning of the text.

Learning Goals

In this lesson, you will learn how writers use transition words to show how two pieces of information are related. You will learn some of the most common transition words and how they are used. You will also learn how to find these words in sentences.

Learn the Skill

Writers will often choose words that help readers see relationships. Relationship words can show cause and effect, addition, comparison, and contrast. Knowing the meanings of these special words can help you understand the text. A relationship word can be in the middle of a sentence joining two phrases or clauses. Or, it can begin a sentence to signal to the reader that a connection is coming.

The following chart lists several common relationship words and their uses. Notice how the information in the example sentences is joined in some way by these words.

Use	Relationship Words
addition	also, furthermore, in addition, moreover
comparison	similarly
contrast	although, but, due to, however, nevertheless
effect	as a result, therefore, so
cause	because, due to

Examples

I ate dinner at the restaurant, and I also had dessert there.

Although I knew the way to the hospital, I made a wrong turn and got lost.

As a result of cutting her finger on broken glass, she needed six stitches.

The flight was delayed because of poor weather conditions.

Example 1

Relationship words signal connections

Look at the relationship between the ideas in this sentence:

It is a bright and sunny day. ***Therefore****, I will walk to work instead of drive.*

The word *therefore* tells you that the second piece of information, "I will walk to work," is an effect of the first part, "It is a bright and sunny day." The word *therefore* in a sentence signals that one event happened as a result of another event.

Here is another example:

Although *it was a bright and sunny day, I decided to drive to work instead of walk.*

In this sentence, the word *although* shows contrast. It is a bright and sunny day and would be a good day to walk to work. The author does the opposite and decides to drive to work.

Read carefully and look for relationship words to understand the author's point.

Example 2

Relationship words can be found in different places in sentences

Read the three sentences below.

As a result *of my high test score, I was offered a scholarship.*
I was offered a scholarship ***as a result*** *of my high test score.*
My test score was high, and I was offered a scholarship ***as a result***.

These sentences show the same relationship: A scholarship was the effect of a person having a high test score. The relationship words *as a result* can be correctly placed in the sentence in many ways.

Workplace Connection

At work, manuals are often given to help workers understand how to use equipment. Understanding relationship words will help you better follow the directions written in the manuals and operate the equipment more safely.

Think

Is the writer adding information, showing cause and effect, or making a comparison? Find the relationship words in the sentence and review the examples in the chart if you are not sure.

Guided Practice

Circle the relationship word(s) in the following sentence. Write down the ideas that the author is connecting and the relationship between them.

1. I bought a bicycle so I could get in shape.

    _____

    _____

    Answer: The relationship word in this sentence is *so*. The two ideas it is connecting are *I bought a bicycle* and *I could get in shape*. Getting in shape is an *effect* of buying the bicycle.

Check for Errors

If you are not sure about which relationship word to choose on a test question, try reading the sentence with each of the answer choices to find the one that makes the most sense.

Independent Practice

Circle the word or phrase in parentheses that best shows the relationship between the two ideas in the sentence.

2. The trip to Hawaii took over 18 hours and cost me $3,000, (*but   in addition   so*) the beauty of the islands made me forget about the time and expense.

3. (*Although   In addition   Because*) most people know that exercise is good for the body, few schedule time for physical activity.

4. She was late for her appointment; (*in addition   nevertheless   because*), she did not drive over the speed limit.

5. Tara ate dinner at 3 p.m. (*although   also   because*) she was hungry.

6. Fernando is a talented singer and a fine actor (*also   however   because*).

7. I would gladly loan you money to buy a house; (*because   so   however*), my bank account is empty.

Lesson Review

In this lesson, you learned to

- find relationship words in sentences,
- understand the meanings of different relationship words,
- understand that relationship words are found in different places in sentences.

Read the paragraph.

Owning a dog can be a rewarding experience, _____ it can also be a costly one. Some items you must buy are food, a collar, a leash, and a license. _____, you may want to purchase bowls for food and water, a bed for your dog, and a few sweaters to keep him warm in the winter. Being a pet owner can be an expensive hobby, _____ your dog will repay you with love and loyalty.

8. Which word <u>best</u> completes the sentence?

Owning a dog can be a rewarding experience, _____ it can also be a costly one.

A. but

B. so

C. due to

D. because

9. Which word <u>best</u> completes the sentence?

Some items you must buy are food, a collar, a leash, and a license. _____, you may want to purchase bowls for food and water, a bed for your dog, and a few sweaters to keep him warm in the winter.

A. But

B. In addition

C. Because

D. As a result

10. Which word <u>best</u> completes the sentence?

Being a pet owner can be an expensive hobby, _____ your dog will repay you with love and loyalty.

A. because

B. but

C. as a result

D. so

Choose the sentence that is written logically and correctly.

11. A. Because the last train left the station at midnight.

B. Although the train left the station at midnight, it was the last train of the night.

C. Because the last train left the station at midnight, we had to leave the party at 11.

D. Also the last train left the station at midnight, and we had to leave the party at 11.

12. A. Although he wanted to get a better job, he never went back to finish his degree.

B. He never went back to school to finish his degree because he wanted a better job.

C. In addition to wanting a better job, he never went back to school to finish his degree.

D. He never went back to school to finish his degree; as a result, he wanted to get a better job.

Answers begin on page 108.

Skill Check

Lesson 1

1. Read the sentence.

   > Louisa was a scrupulous reporter. She based her actions at work on what she thought was right.

   Based on context clues, what is the most likely definition of *scrupulous*?

   A. being extremely competitive

   B. acting carelessly

   C. having strict ethical or moral standards

   D. acting very quickly

2. Which sentence has a contrast-type context clue for the word *glean*?

   A. He tried to read through the data to glean some insights, but he was unable to gather any information.

   B. He read through the data to glean insights. Bit by bit, he gathered a lot of information.

   C. He read the data to glean insights and discovered that sales had increased slowly over time.

   D. To *glean* means to learn or discover little by little.

3. What is the suffix in the word *sustainable*?

   A. sus-

   B. sustain-

   C. ain

   D. -able

4. Read the sentence.

   > Ren loves to study aquatic animals.

   Based on its prefix, what is the most likely definition of *aquatic*?

   A. having four legs

   B. having two fins

   C. living or growing in water

   D. living or growing on land

5. If you want to look for synonyms for the word *remarkable*, which kind of resource should you use?

   A. a dictionary

   B. a thesaurus

   C. a cookbook

   D. an encyclopedia

Lesson 2

6. Read the paragraph.

   > Earthquakes are a shaking of the earth's surface. They happen at fault lines. Seismic waves are sent in many directions from the epicenter of the earthquake. Earthquakes can be felt over large areas. Scientists use seismographs to measure the intensity of earthquakes.

   Underline the topic words.

7. Read the paragraph.

> Amelia Earhart was the first woman to fly as a passenger across the Atlantic Ocean. In 1921, she got her U.S. flying license. In 1922, she set an altitude record for women of 14,000 feet.

Which sentence below uses the word *altitude* correctly?

A. Today, female pilots make altitudes all the time.

B. On certain nights, you can see great altitudes in the sky without a telescope.

C. You have to complete many practice driving hours before reaching altitude in a car.

D. Sometimes even experienced hikers take a while to adjust to high altitudes.

8. Read the sentences.

> Oranges are a major export of the state of Florida. They grow better in Florida than in the other states that buy them.

Which sentence below uses the word *export* correctly?

A. Ireland is not able to produce all of its own airplanes, so it exports a lot of them.

B. The farmers of the region grow barley and wheat, which are valuable exports to other markets.

C. The town needs to keep all of its cotton to make clothing, so they export it.

D. Several countries export their towns in order to grow.

Read the paragraph. Then answer questions 9–11.

Building Blocks of Matter

The basic building block of all matter is the atom. Atoms have three parts: protons, neutrons, and electrons. Protons are positively charged particles that are found in the nucleus, or control center, of the atom. Neutrons have no electric charge and are also found in the nucleus. Electrons have a negative charge. They are are found in areas called shells, or orbitals, which surround the nucleus.

9. What is the subject of this paragraph?

A. orbitals

B. protons

C. neutrons

D. atoms

10. Protons, neutrons, and electrons are all particles that make up atoms. What does the word part *pro-* probably mean?

A. center

B. negative

C. building block

D. positive

11. List the topic words from the paragraph.

_____

_____

_____

Lesson 3

12. Read the paragraph.

> Rodrigo signed up to run a marathon next summer. He made a training schedule in addition to a new eating plan. He even bought new running shoes. Furthermore, he is planning to start a blog to track his progress. Although he has never run a race that long, he hopes that he will be able to do it!

Underline the relationship words.

13. Read the sentence.

> Daria dropped her cell phone and had to pay for the screen to be repaired as a result.

What ideas does the phrase *as a result* connect?

_____

_____

14. Which word <u>best</u> completes the following sentence?

> Painting a room on your own may take a lot of time and effort, _____ it can save a lot of money.

A. and

B. so

C. because

D. but

15. Which word or phrase <u>best</u> completes the following sentence?

> The napkins blew away from the picnic blanket _____ the strong winds.

A. due to

B. in addition to

C. nevertheless

D. although

16. Which sentence is written correctly?

A. I was really nervous to submit my application, so I went through with it as a result.

B. Due to being really nervous to submit my application, I went through with it.

C. I was really nervous to submit my application; nevertheless, I went through with it.

D. I was really nervous to submit my application, and I went through with it.

Answers begin on page 108.

UNIT 3

Write Different Text Types

This unit will cover the following topics:

- Writing opinion pieces
- Writing information pieces

Analyn is an administrative assistant. She is responsible for taking notes at company meetings. The day after the meeting she writes a report about the meeting. The report is sent to everyone who was at the meeting.

Studying about writing informational texts has helped Analyn to organize information for the report more clearly. The company president has praised her improved work. The president said Analyn's reports include more relevant facts, definitions of uncommon words, and concrete details about what was discussed in the meetings. She especially likes that Analyn includes quotations from the participants in the report. All of this helps the company, the president told Analyn.

Write Opinion Pieces

Vocabulary

- introduction
- conclusion
- logical

Learning Goals

In this lesson, you will learn how to identify introductions and conclusions in an opinion piece. You will learn how to tell the difference between facts and opinions. You will learn to recognize logical reasons. Then, you will learn how to find and use certain words to link opinions to reasons.

Learn the Skill

A good opinion piece has more than just a writer's opinions. It has reasons that explain those opinions. It also has plenty of facts to support those opinions. Keep your audience in mind when you write an opinion piece. Use words and sentences that readers will understand and like.

A good opinion piece begins with an **introduction**. This should include a topic sentence that tells the reader what the piece is about. It should also state the writer's opinion.

Readers should be able to tell facts from opinions. They should also be able to notice the reasons for the writer's opinions.

Certain words should be used in opinion pieces to show how the opinions are linked with the ideas. These linking words include *specifically*, *in particular*, and *to illustrate*.

Finally, opinion pieces should have **conclusions**. These should paraphrase, or restate in different words, the opinions and support them with reasons.

Example 1

Introduction

Read this example introduction to an opinion piece:

> Some towns are better than others. I think Smithville is better than Jonesville for many reasons.

The first sentence gives the topic of the piece. It provides focus. It lets readers know that the piece will discuss why one town is better than another.

The second sentence gives the writer's opinion. She thinks Smithville is better than Jonesville.

Sometimes the topic and opinion are combined into one sentence, like this:

> While some towns are better than others, I think Smithville and Jonesville are both great.

Introductions can also be several sentences long. In the following introduction, the first three sentences give the topic. The final sentence gives the writer's opinion.

> People have been comparing towns for years. Some people focus on jobs. Other people focus on houses. I think parks are the most important part of a town.

Note that many introductions include both facts and opinions. The first three sentences in the introduction above are facts. The last sentence is an opinion.

Workplace Connection

When writing for work, keep your audience in mind. If you work in a medical lab, for example, you will want to use medical language in your writing. This would not be the case if you worked in a factory.

Think

Try to include important facts and data in your supporting reasons. Be sure these come from good sources. Personal experiences are facts, but they are usually not as powerful as good data.

Don't Forget

Although opinion pieces are a more personal form of writing, they should still have proper grammar and spelling. Check your writing using the writing checklists you made in other lessons.

Example 2

Supporting Reasons

After stating the topic and her opinion, the writer should explain why she has that opinion. She should support her opinion with reasons. This includes information and facts that support the opinion. Here is an example of an introduction followed by reasons:

> While some towns are better than others, I think Smithville and Jonesville are both great.
>
> Smithville has the top-rated schools in the state. It also has some of the cheapest homes in the county. Jonesville, meanwhile, recently won an award for beautiful parks. It also has some of the top restaurants in the area.

Notice that the reasons are in a **logical** order. That means they appear in a sensible order. In this case, all the great things about Smithville are stated. Then all the great things about Jonesville are stated. It would not be logical to state one good thing about Smithville, one good thing about Jonesville, another good thing about Smithville, etc.

Putting things in a logical order makes things easier to read.

Linking words can be used to connect opinions to reasons. Here is an example:

> While some towns are better than others, I think Smithville and Jonesville are both great.
>
> To illustrate, Smithville has the top-rated schools in the state. It also has some of the most affordable homes in the county. Jonesville, meanwhile, has beautiful parks. Specifically, Willow Park won an award for being the most popular park in the state.

Example 3

Conclusion

The conclusion of an opinion piece appears at the end. It is usually short. Conclusions should paraphrase the writer's opinion. That means they should state the writer's opinion again with different words. A conclusion can also include another supporting reason. Here is an example:

> The residents of both Smithville and Jonesville have no reason to be jealous of each other. Both towns are incredible for different reasons. And let's not forget: Our region has one of the nicest climates in North America!

Notice that the writer uses the word *incredible* here instead of *great*. This is an example of using different words to convey the same message. The writer also adds a supporting reason: both towns have beautiful climates.

Guided Practice

Read the sentences. They include a topic sentence, an opinion, and two supporting reasons. Which sentence should be moved to correct the sentence order? On the line below, write the sentence numbers in the correct order.

1. (1) This is why I think high school classes should start later. (2) Science has shown that teenagers need extra sleep. (3) Two hours of extra sleep will have students ready to learn! (4) Specifically, our 7:00 a.m. start time should be moved to 9:00 a.m.

    _____

2. Which of these sentences is a statement of fact?

    _____

    _____

    Answers: The order should be 2, 1, 3, 4. Sentence 2 is a statement of fact. Sentence 2 is the topic sentence and should be first. Sentence 1 is the writer's main opinion and should be second. Sentences 3 and 4 should remain where they are. They provide reasons for the opinion.

Independent Practice

Choose whether each sentence is an example of a topic introduction, an opinion, a supporting reason, or a conclusion.

3. This painting, in particular, shows that Picasso was the greatest artist of his time.

    A. topic introduction

    B. opinion

    C. supporting reason

    D. conclusion

4. Once again, I want to state that Pat Lee is the best choice for mayor.

    A. topic introduction

    B. opinion

    C. supporting reason

    D. conclusion

Real-World Connection

You may not realize it, but you have probably written opinion pieces before. Think of all the emails you have written. Think of the things you have posted on social media. What you learn in this lesson can help with those types of writing too.

Test Tip

Be careful when deciding whether something is a fact or an opinion. A statement is not a fact just because most people agree with it. This is an opinion: *California has the nicest weather of all the states.* This is a fact: *Yuma, Arizona has the most sunny days of any major city in the United States.*

5. Hiking has become one of the most popular activities in the world.

   A. topic introduction

   B. opinion

   C. supporting reason

   D. conclusion

Read the sentences below. Choose the answer that puts the sections in the best order. Then choose the best explanation for this order.

1) Let me state again that stopping this fish from spreading is critical. If it gets into the Great Lakes, our most important source of fresh water could be damaged.

2) The Asian carp is a large fish that has spread throughout the Mississippi River and other rivers. We must do everything we can to prevent it from spreading further.

3) The Asian carp can injure people too. To illustrate, this fish can jump several feet into the air. It does this when frightened by loud boats. Several people have been injured by jumping carp.

4) The Asian carp invades areas where other fish live. This causes great destruction. In particular, it destroys the plants that other fish need to survive. Many other fish are dying.

6. What is the <u>best</u> order?

   A. 1, 2, 3, 4

   B. 4, 3, 2, 1

   C. 2, 4, 3, 1

   D. 3, 4, 1, 2

7. Why should section 4 appear before section 3?

   A. Section 4 is more important than section 3.

   B. Section 3 fits better before the conclusion.

   C. The word too in section 3 shows that this should come after section 4.

   D. The phrase *to illustrate* in section 3 shows that this should come after section 4.

Lesson Review

In this lesson, you learned to

- tell the difference between fact and opinion;
- begin opinion writing with an introduction and topic sentence, then state an opinion and reason for writing;
- use certain words to show how opinions are linked with reasons;
- use a conclusion to paraphrase the opinion and support it with reasons.

Read the opinion piece.

Studies show that kids leave their houses much less often than they used to. I think schools should open their gyms on weekends for recreation and other activities.

This would allow kids to get more exercise. Specifically, they could play basketball, work out, or just walk around the gym.

This would also give kids time to socialize with each other in person. Kids spend too much time on their devices. More face-to-face time will help their social skills.

8. What is the topic of this piece?

   A. Kids are getting into too much trouble.

   B. Kids leave their houses much less often now.

   C. Schools should open their gyms for kids on weekends.

   D. Kids should spend more time socializing.

9. What is the writer's main opinion?

   A. Kids are getting into too much trouble.

   B. Kids leave their houses much less often now.

   C. Schools should open their gyms for kids on weekends.

   D. Kids should spend more time socializing.

10. The piece is missing a conclusion. Which of these paraphrases the original opinion?

    A. I also think schools should do a better job cleaning up the trash on their grounds.

    B. I know this will be expensive, but I'm sure it could be paid for with donations.

    C. What do you say, schools? Open your doors on weekends and help kids become healthier and happier!

    D. I encourage everyone to contact the school district to find out if this is possible.

11. Which of these would be the <u>best</u> supporting reason to add to this piece?

    A. The recreation would help kids become healthier.

    B. One challenge would be to pay people to staff these events.

    C. This would be a good way for teachers to earn extra money.

    D. Schools should also provide after-school daycare for busy parents.

12. Which one of these sentences is a statement of fact?

    A. I think schools should open their gyms on weekends for recreation and other activities.

    B. Kids spend too much time on their devices.

    C. More face-to-face time will help their social skills.

    D. Studies show that kids leave their houses much less often than they used to.

Answers begin on page 109.

Write Information Pieces

Vocabulary

- concrete details
- inferences
- generalizations
- domain-specific language

Learning Goals

In this lesson, you will learn how to identify introductory topic sentences in information pieces. You will learn how to use precise, academic, and domain-specific language. You will learn how to develop topics with facts, definitions, concrete details, quotations, and examples. Finally, you will learn how to identify conclusions, some with inferences and generalizations.

Learn the Skill

Information pieces give ideas and facts about a topic. The introduction should have a clear topic sentence. You should use precise language to help readers understand exactly what you mean.

The body and conclusion of a text are just as important as the introduction. The body should have different kinds of supporting information. This includes facts, definitions, concrete details, quotations, and examples. You should use words to link ideas within categories. Such linking words include *another*, *for example*, *also*, and *because*.

The conclusion of an information piece should be related to the main topic. It should summarize the main idea. Inferences and generalizations are often included.

Example 1

Introduction

Information pieces should begin with an introduction. Be sure to use precise language when introducing your topic. This makes it easy for readers to follow. Below is an example of an introduction. The topic sentence is underlined.

> Commercial fishers have many ways of catching fish. <u>Gillnetting is one of the most popular ways.</u> It is very effective. It is also responsible. When done right, gillnetting does not cause a lot of bycatch. This means it does not kill many other fish.

This topic sentence lets readers know that the piece will be about gillnetting specifically. It is not about other fishing methods. It is not about fish in general.

This precise topic sentence allows readers to choose whether to read the piece or not. Maybe they will choose not to read this because they already know about this topic. Such readers will be grateful that you clearly stated your topic in your introduction.

Below are some examples of general language and precise language. Precise language usually needs fewer words to express meaning. This makes it easier to read.

Examples of general language	Examples of specific language
Place a sheet on the floor when painting to avoid a mess.	Use a drop cloth when painting to avoid a mess.
The people who were hiking slept in a simple wooden structure in the woods.	The hikers slept in a cabin.
That is the person who fixes our pipes when they are clogged.	That is the plumber.

Workplace Connection

It is often best to use simple words in the workplace. For example, use *try* rather than *endeavor*. Compare these sentences: *I will* try *to finish before midnight. I will* endeavor *to finish before midnight.* Nearly everyone will understand the word *try*. Some people might not understand *endeavor*.

Example 2

Body

After you introduce your topic, use the body of the text to support it. You can support your topic with facts, definitions, concrete details, quotations, or examples. A combination of these is often best.

Below is another paragraph from the information piece on gillnetting. It supports the piece's topic with facts, concrete details, and examples.

> Gillnetting is simple. Only one or two people are needed to catch hundreds of fish. The net is made of a thin line that many fish can't see. Some nets have bigger holes. Some have smaller holes. It depends on the kind of fish the fishers want. This net is stretched across the water for several hundred yards. The top of the net floats. The bottom of the net sinks. This forms a kind of "net wall." Some fish get stuck in the net. Smaller fish, such as minnows, swim through the holes. Bigger fish, such as sharks, push into the net and back away.

Information pieces often have academic or domain-specific vocabulary. **Domain-specific language** is related to a specific field, such as dentistry, information technology, welding, or nursing.

You have to be careful when using this kind of vocabulary. If your readers know the words, they will be able to understand the meaning. But if your readers don't know the words, they may become frustrated. Always think about who will be reading your writing.

Look at this sentence from the paragraph above: *The net is made of a thin line that many fish can't see.*

With domain-specific vocabulary, that sentence might look like this: *The net is made of a transparent monofilament.*

Which sentence is better? That depends on who your readers are. If your readers are commercial fishers, then the second sentence would probably be best. If your readers are other people, then the first sentence might be better.

Examples of common language	Examples of domain-specific language
You should store your electronic files in a system outside your computer that you can access from anywhere.	You should store your electronic files in the cloud.
Lawrence wants to be a person who helps a dentist work on people's teeth.	Lawrence wants to be a dental hygienist.
We are going to plant flowers that will return every year.	We are going to plant perennials.

Example 3

Conclusion

The conclusion of a piece must be related to its main topic. It should summarize the main idea. It may also contain a generalization or inference.

> Gillnetting is useful because just one or two people can catch hundreds of fish. Another advantage of gillnetting is that it does not produce much bycatch. In the future, more fishers will likely be using this method.

The first two sentences above summarize the topic. The third sentence is a generalization. This conclusion also has several linking words. This type of word includes *another*, *for example*, *also*, and *because*. These words help connect ideas within categories. In the sample conclusion above, *because* and *another* are used to link gillnetting with positive outcomes.

Don't Forget

You learned about certain linking words in the Writing Opinion Pieces lesson. These words include *specifically*, *in particular*, and *to illustrate*. These words work equally well with information pieces. All of these words can be used to connect ideas throughout your text.

Think

You have learned how to use context to help you understand new words when reading. When you're writing, you can use some of those same tricks. Provide synonyms, explanations, or examples for words that might be new to your readers.

Check for Errors

Sometimes our ideas change as we're writing. We learn new things. We make new connections. We develop new thoughts. Always re-read your writing before submitting it. Check to make sure your original topic sentence still fits. Sometimes you'll need to change your topic sentence to fit your new ideas.

Guided Practice

Read the paragraph below. Underline the topic sentence. Circle the domain-specific words.

> This piece will explain the proper way to brush your teeth. You will learn what kind of toothpaste to use. You will learn how to hold your toothbrush. And you will learn how to brush your front teeth, your bicuspids, and your molars.

Answers: The first sentence is the topic sentence. The domain-specific words are *bicuspids* and *molars*. If you are writing to a general audience, you might not want to use these terms. *Toothpaste*, *toothbrush*, and *front teeth* are general terms. You can expect most people to know these words.

Independent Practice

The sentences below are from an article on ticks. Choose the best description for each sentence.

2. *This article will discuss several ways to protect yourself against ticks.*
   A. This is probably part of the article's conclusion.
   B. This sentence has a supporting example.
   C. This sentence has a supporting fact.
   D. This is probably a topic sentence.

3. *First, always tuck your pant legs into your socks.*
   A. This is probably part of the article's conclusion.
   B. This sentence has a supporting quote.
   C. This is the beginning of a list.
   D. This is probably a topic sentence.

4. *Another option is to wear clothing treated with permethrin.*
   A. This is probably part of the article's conclusion.
   B. This sentence has domain-specific language.
   C. This sentence has a supporting quote.
   D. This is probably a topic sentence.

5. *Your insect repellent should contain at least 20% DEET.*
   A. This is probably part of the article's conclusion.
   B. This sentence has a supporting example.
   C. This sentence has a supporting quote.
   D. This sentence has concrete details.

6. *All of these methods can keep ticks from biting you.*
   A. This is probably part of the article's conclusion.
   B. This is probably a topic sentence.
   C. This sentence has domain-specific vocabulary.
   D. This sentence has concrete details.

7. *"You should avoid areas where deer live," said Ranger Eva Smith.*
   A. This is probably part of the article's conclusion.
   B. This is probably a topic sentence.
   C. This sentence has domain-specific vocabulary.
   D. This sentence has a supporting quote.

Lesson Review

In this lesson, you learned to

- identify an introduction that includes a topic sentence;
- identify and use precise language;
- identify and use academic and domain-specific words;
- develop topics with facts, definitions, concrete details, quotations, and examples;
- identify a conclusion that draws inferences or makes generalizations.

Read the information piece.

(1) Harriet Tubman was an important figure in American history. (2) She played key roles as an abolitionist and a suffragette.

(3) Tubman was born into slavery in Maryland. (4) She escaped from slavery in 1849. (5) She returned to Maryland 13 times and helped 70 other slaves escape. (6) During the U.S. Civil War, she was a scout and spy for the United States Army.

(7) Later, Tubman worked to get women the right to vote. (8) She traveled to New York City, Boston, and Washington, D.C., to give speeches for women's suffrage.

8. Which sentence has the topic of the piece?

   A. 1

   B. 3

   C. 5

   D. 7

9. Which three sentences contain concrete details that support the topic?

   A. 3

   B. 5

   C. 6

   D. 8

10. Which sentence has academic vocabulary?

    A. 1

    B. 2

    C. 3

    D. 4

11. The piece is missing a conclusion. Which of these would be the best conclusion?

    A. Tubman overcame many obstacles in her life.

    B. Tubman lived through one of the most interesting times in history.

    C. Tubman played key roles in two major events in U.S. history.

    D. Tubman was one of the most courageous people ever.

Answers begin on page 109.

Skill Check

Lesson 1

1. Which is the <u>best</u> topic sentence for an opinion essay on air travel?

   A. Airplanes first flew at Kitty Hawk, N.C.

   B. Some people are afraid to fly.

   C. Airplanes are the best way to get from place to place.

   D. People can travel by ship, airplane, car, and train.

2. Read the sentences.

   Many people treat their dogs like children.

   Which is the best choice for the next sentence?

   A. Consequently, the market for dog products is growing.

   B. Otherwise, the market for dog products is growing.

   C. Secondly, the market for dog products is growing.

   D. Perhaps the market for dog products is growing.

3. Read the sentence.

   Children benefit greatly from growing their own food.

   Which sentence is the best conclusion to an opinion piece with this topic?

   A. Healthy eating is important, especially to growing children.

   B. The many benefits children get from growing their own food make it worth the effort.

   C. Children in the city may have a harder time growing their own food.

   D. Growing food requires a lot of energy and time.

4. Read the paragraph.

   Therefore, high school students should never have to start school before 9 a.m. Studies show teenagers need more sleep. Early morning high school start times can be tough on teenagers. Their body clocks are set to a nighttime schedule.

   Rewrite the sentences in the correct order for an introduction paragraph.

   _____

   _____

   _____

   _____

   _____

5. Read the sentence.

   When developing a menu, be careful because many people have food allergies.

   Which is the best choice for the next sentence?

   A. Therefore, try to avoid peanuts and other common allergy triggers.

   B. Nevertheless, try to avoid peanuts and other common allergy triggers.

   C. Likewise, try to avoid peanuts and other common allergy triggers.

   D. Similarly, try to avoid peanuts and other common allergy triggers.

6. Read the thesis statement.

   Always hire a professional for electrical work in your home.

   What is a logical supporting reason for this opinion?

   A. Electricians need to earn a living so you should support them.

   B. Plumbing and carpentry are jobs you can do yourself.

   C. Electrical work can be very dangerous if you aren't trained.

   D. Professionals always clean up their mess when they are done.

7. Which of the following statements is an opinion?

   A. Cellphones in schools should be limited because they are distracting.

   B. Many schools do not allow cellphones in class.

   C. Some schools use cellphones as learning tools.

   D. Cellphone use in schools is rising.

8. Read the paragraph.

   Also, it can be very relaxing. You get a change of scenery. Travel can be very rewarding. Everyone should try to travel at least once a year. Secondly, you can learn about other cultures.

   Rewrite the sentences in the correct order for an introduction paragraph.

   _____

   _____

   _____

   _____

   _____

Lesson 2

9. Which sentence is the <u>best</u> choice for a biology paper?

   A. More people have brown eyes than blue eyes because of genes.

   B. Blue eyes are appealing because their genes aren't as common.

   C. If your parents have the gene for blue eyes, you may have them, too.

   D. Blue eyes are recessive, which means both parents must have the gene for blue eyes or their children will not have them.

10. Read the sentence.

    Written communication has changed greatly over time.

    Which fact best fits this topic?

    A. People also communicate orally.

    B. The oldest known written language is Sumerian.

    C. Many people know more than one written language.

    D. Writing is a challenge for some students.

11. What is the purpose of a conclusion in an informational essay?

    A. It reminds the reader of the topic.

    B. It adds new, important details to the topic.

    C. It draws inferences or makes generalizations about the topic.

    D. It gives the author's opinion on the topic.

12. Which is the best topic sentence?

   A. Different ecosystems support different flora and fauna.

   B. A savannah is a grassy ecosystem.

   C. The Earth is home to many different ecosystems.

   D. Many ecosystems can be found on one continent.

13. Read the sentence.

   Artists often express themselves through their work.

   Which quotation best supports the statement?

   A. "I often paint when I can't find words to say how I feel."

   B. "Painting is fun for me, so I like to do it often."

   C. "When I paint, I don't think about other things."

   D. "I paint because the finished work makes good presents."

14. Read the paragraph.

   Algorithms are important when doing math. They make it easier to do the same thing more than once. Being able to use algorithms is an important skill. Many scientists have created algorithms to predict changes in climate or weather.

   What would be a good addition to this paragraph?

   A. A definition of algorithm.

   B. An example of an algorithm.

   C. An argument for the use of algorithms.

   D. A conclusion about algorithms.

15. Read the paragraph.

   One example of an individual activity anyone can try is marathon running. A marathon is 26.2 miles. Running a marathon requires training and dedication. The fastest runners finish in a little more than 2 hours, but the average time is 4–5 hours. With some dedication, many people will be able to complete a marathon, but they will be running for far longer than the winners.

   Which is the best heading for this paragraph?

   A. Marathon Training

   B. Amateurs Can't Win Marathons

   C. Two-hour Marathons

   D. An Activity for Almost Anyone

Answers begin on page 109.

TABE Test Practice

1. Read the sentences.

   > Plants use photosynthesis. Without sunlight, they would run out of food.

   What does the word *photosynthesis* mean?

   A. using light from the sun to make food

   B. turning toward the sun

   C. eating food they find in the daytime

   D. digesting food from the earth

2. Read the paragraph.

   > (1) Karen wanted to go to the dance party, but she was self-conscience. (2) She said she had no rhythm. (3) Her friend gave her seperate lessons before the party. (4) After that, she felt that she definitly would not embbarrass herself.

   Which sentence is written correctly?

   A. 1

   B. 2

   C. 3

   D. 4

3. Which sentence is written correctly?

   A. My dog was barking every time someone walks by.

   B. I will be on a phone call yesterday.

   C. The interview is happening right now.

   D. He was practicing next Tuesday for the debate.

4. Read the paragraph.

   > A trainer must do the same thing every time the animal behaves a certain way. Rewarding good behavior reinforces it. After some time, the animal will learn how the trainer expects it to act.

   The paragraph is missing an introduction. Which of the sentences would best introduce the topic?

   A. Some animals are not trained.

   B. Training animals requires patience and consistency.

   C. Without training, animals will not listen.

   D. Animals enjoy being trained so they know how to act.

5. Which sentence is written correctly?

   A. He likes neither hot dogs or hamburgers.

   B. My mom works both in our home and at an office job.

   C. We can either go to the park and the beach.

   D. The teacher asked us to use both blue or black ink.

6. Read the paragraph.

   Consumers should look at more than prices when they shop. Sometimes, very large companies take advantage of workers. They drive down wages and only hire part-time workers. This means people need to have more than one job. They may not have health insurance or other benefits.

   This paragraph is missing a conclusion. Which sentence would best conclude the paragraph?

   A. I think prices are important, but so are other issues.

   B. Sometimes, you just have to buy the cheapest item.

   C. Always shop local, because it is way better.

   D. Prices should not be a consumer's only consideration when shopping.

7. Which sentence is punctuated correctly?

   A. "Mom, will you take me shopping later, I asked?"

   B. My professor said that "we will have a 10-page paper to write."

   C. "Actually," I said, "I would like a turkey sandwich."

   D. The real estate agent said "I have just the right house for you."

8. Which sentence is written correctly?

   A. I was running up the hill, then I fell.

   B. The movie was great, you should see it.

   C. I volunteer at the pet shelter and love it.

   D. My son at school.

9. Which sentence is written correctly?

   A. Our new apartment has four small, rectangular bedrooms.

   B. For the party, we need helium, purple, round balloons.

   C. There are metal, yellow, many chairs in the auditorium.

   D. The library offers a new, large collection of audio books.

10. Read the paragraph.

    (1) Roses are a prized flower in many gardens and can be beautiful with a little care. (2) In order to grow, roses need at least six hours a day of sunshine. (3) Roses should not be watered frequently. (4) The bushes grow best in soil that drains well and is rich in nutrients. (5) Roses also need regular pruning, or cutting back. (5) There are many varieties and colors of roses. (6) The ones you choose to plant are a matter of your own taste.

    Read the sentence.

    Also, the water should be applied directly to the soil.

    Where should the sentence be placed in the paragraph?

    A. after sentence 2

    B. after sentence 3

    C. after sentence 4

    D. after sentence 5

11. Which sentence is written correctly?

    A. Try moving the internet router to when it is closer to the modem.

    B. The reason why I want a new coat is that mine is too small.

    C. Remember the time where you ate too much ice cream?

    D. The house is safe where the alarm is set.

12. Read the paragraph.

Many people believe buying a house is always better than renting, but it is not. Home ownership is a big responsibility. Repairs can be expensive and time-consuming. Also, houses do not always go up in value. That means they may not be a good investment. Renters don't have to pay for repairs. They can also move without worrying about selling a house.

The paragraph is missing a conclusion. Which sentence would best conclude the paragraph?

A. Home ownership is a responsibility, and people should think hard about before choosing it.

B. It is better to own a house if you don't mind doing repairs.

C. It is always better to rent a place to live because renters don't have to be responsible.

D. There are pluses and minuses to both homeownership and renting.

13. Read the sentences.

One day, I decided to take my children to the art museum. They love taking the train, so we did. _____, it would have been a very long walk.

The last sentence is missing a relationship word. Which of these would best complete the sentence?

A. Furthermore

B. Therefore

C. Nevertheless

D. Although

14. Read the paragraph.

(1) There are many ways to study for a test. (2) One good way is to use flash cards. (3) You can create flash cards online or use paper cards. (4) It is not enough to just look at the flash cards. (5) Studying with flash cards helps you learn and remember better than just re-reading your notes.

Read the sentence.

Try placing the flash cards into logical categories as you think about them.

Where should the sentence be placed in the paragraph?

A. before sentence 2

B. before sentence 3

C. before sentence 1

D. before sentence 5

15. Which sentence includes an example of dialect?

A. He uses Spanish words as well as English words.

B. This concrete jungle ain't no good for no one.

C. My mom used to call me "Pumpkin."

D. I have a hard time understanding Southern accents.

16. Which sentence is written using formal language?

A. Please inform the committee that I cannot attend the meeting Monday.

B. My buddy won't be able to come to my party.

C. His dog escaped and, wow, was it hard to catch her!

D. The kid hid behind the counter when the clown showed up.

17. Which sentence is written correctly?

   A. The boy is to old too go to preschool.

   B. Please bring you're laptop to there conference.

   C. They're going to come to your performance.

   D. The movers dropped you're desk and lamp, two.

Read the paragraph. Then answer questions 18–20.

Carpentry Tools

Carpenters work with wood to build many things, such as furniture or even whole houses. They use a variety of tools. A tape measure helps them figure out the exact size they need. Then they might use a saw to cut a piece of wood to that size. A nail gun can save a lot of time because it places nails quickly and without a lot of energy. Another important tool is a level, which helps determine whether a board is slanted or not. Finally, none of these tools would be very useful without a work bench to place them on.

18. Which sentence uses the word *level* correctly?

   A. When I put up a shelf, I used a level to make sure it was straight.

   B. A level saved me a lot of energy when I was building a birdhouse.

   C. I needed a level to tell whether I was cutting the wood to the correct size.

   D. I almost cut myself while using the level.

19. Which sentence uses the words *nail gun* correctly?

   A. A nail gun saved me from pounding with a hammer.

   B. The directions said to use a nail gun to check the size of the window.

   C. I used a nail gun to cut a piece for my wooden boat.

   D. The nail gun was just the right height for me to work easily.

20. Which sentence uses the word *saw* correctly?

   A. After measuring with a saw, the wood can be cut.

   B. Saws make it easy to secure wood with many nails.

   C. A saw cuts wood by using a back-and-forth motion.

   D. It is helpful to put all the tools on the saw for easy access.

21. Which sentence is written correctly?

   A. We went to the Lake to have a picnic last Weekend.

   B. On Thanksgiving Day, we ate delicious turkey and watched football.

   C. The club President and Chairperson attended the conference.

   D. His Speech was on the topic of Improving Education in the city.

22. Read the paragraph.

   (1) Three different people recommended the next book our book club should read. (2) I said we should read *Jazz by Toni Morrison*. (3) Another member thought we should try "Americanah" by Chimamanda Ngozi Adichie. (4) The third wanted to choose *Lord of the Flies* by William Golding, because his son was reading it for class. (5) We decided on a fourth book, "Pachinko by Min Jin Lee," after a long discussion.

   Which sentence is written correctly?

   A. 2

   B. 3

   C. 4

   D. 5

23. Which sentence is punctuated correctly?

A. When, I want to relax, I listen to classical music, with my eyes closed.

B. Yes, after I eat dinner, I would like to go to a movie at the mall.

C. The class had a choice of, writing a paper, making a video, or creating a slide show.

D. Business partners, do best if they understand each other's strengths and weaknesses.

24. Read the paragraph.

Asia is the biggest continent in terms of area. It is more than 17 million square miles. With a population of 4.4 billion, it is also home to the most people. This huge land mass also contains Mount Everest, the highest point on Earth, and the Dead Sea, the lowest point on Earth. One statistic in which Asia comes in second is number of countries. It has 48. Africa has the most with 54.

The paragraph is missing an introduction. Which of these sentences would best introduce the topic?

A. The Earth is made up of seven continents, but Asia is No. 1.

B. Asia is the best continent for many reasons.

C. You should visit Asia if you want to go to a great place.

D. Of the seven continents, Asia ranks No. 1 in many categories.

25. Read the paragraph.

The human body contains 206 bones in adulthood. This does not include the three tiny bones in each ear. With those, people have 212 bones. When babies are born, they have 270–300 bones. Some of the bones grow together, or fuse, as we grow.

Which example would best support the topic?

A. The bone most likely to get broken is the collarbone.

B. Calcium and vitamin D are necessary for healthy bones.

C. Humans also have more than 100 muscles, tendons, and ligaments.

D. Each hand contains 27 separate bones.

26. Read the paragraph.

(1) The Titanic, a passenger ship built in Britain, was supposed to be unsinkable. (2) However, in 1912, it hit an iceberg in the freezing Atlantic Ocean on its first trip and did sink. (3) About 1,500 people died. (4) Margaret "Molly" Brown was a survivor of the sinking and helped command a lifeboat during the disaster. (5) She was able to help many survivors because she spoke several languages. (6) Margaret Brown was a socialite and was one of the first woman to run for political office. (7) In 1932, she was given the French Legion of Honor partly because she helped during the Titanic disaster. (8) She became known as "The Unsinkable Molly Brown" after her death.

Which sentence should be removed because it contains unnecessary or distracting information?

A. 3

B. 4

C. 5

D. 6

27. Which sentence is written logically and correctly?

    A. The campers like to play soccer, also not volleyball.

    B. Although he is hungry, he will eat a hot dog.

    C. I am going to drive, however, I have my license.

    D. Similar to strawberries, raspberries are a red fruit.

28. Which sentence is written correctly?

    A. I don't think I can accomodate all the necessary equipment.

    B. Take your car in for maintnance on a regular skedule.

    C. The seashell is a momento of your special occassion.

    D. I am definitely going to make an appearance in the play.

29. Read the paragraph.

    Animals should not be kept in zoos. Zoos are too small, especially for large animals that travel long distances in the wild. If scientists want to study animals, they should go to the animals' habitat whenever possible. If animals are sick or need care, then it is acceptable to keep them with humans who can help them.

    This paragraph is missing a conclusion. Which of these would best conclude the paragraph?

    A. Animals must not be kept in captivity unless they need help from humans for a short time.

    B. Zoos are not fun places to visit because the animals are probably not happy.

    C. Zoos can be educational for people if they read the information on the cages.

    D. Maybe people who like zoos should be put into cages and they will change their minds.

30. Read the sentences.

    When Joshua got into the rowboat, it started rocking hard. In fact, it was rocking so much, he was afraid it would capsize.

    What does the word *capsize* mean?

    A. leave

    B. speed up

    C. get stuck

    D. tip over

31. Read the paragraph.

    (1) In the summer, I decided to take a painting class. (2) It was the first art class I had ever taken. (3) The teacher of the class said that anyone could learn to paint. (4) I was nervous, but after the first few classes, I got better.

    Which sentence does not contain a prepositional phrase?

    A. 1

    B. 2

    C. 3

    D. 4

32. Which sentence is written in formal language?

    A. I just gotta get outta this heat right now.

    B. I'm going to take a quick dip in the pool.

    C. My instructor has asked why my essay was not completed on Tuesday.

    D. Don't ask me to help you because I am up to here with work.

33. Read the paragraph.

(1) I will be going on vacation during the winter. (2) Before I went, I have to buy a new winter coat. (3) I did not have one because I live near the equator. (4) I really want to learn to ski, so I am preparing for the cold.

Which sentence is *not* written correctly?

A. 1

B. 2

C. 3

D. 4

34. Which sentence is written correctly to include an example of dialect?

A. I'm fixing to put the book up so it's out of the way.

B. The tech support person had a thick accent and I couldn't understand her.

C. Whenever we go out to eat, I always want to go to a taqueria.

D. Sometimes I think my cat is speaking her own language when she meows.

35. Which sentence is written correctly?

A. "Hey," my friend asked, "will you help me with my essay?"

B. In the nature show, the lion "roared" when it saw a giraffe.

C. My son said that he "can't help me with the chores today."

D. "You will have to stay late to finish the work" my boss said.

36. Read the paragraph.

(1) My family is planning a road trip across the States. (2) My Brother Dylan wants to go to Nashville, Tenn. (3) My sister said she wants to see the Grand Canyon in Arizona. (4) I have never been to the Ocean, so I want to go to the beach in California.

Which sentence is written correctly?

A. 1

B. 2

C. 3

D. 4

37. Which sentence is written correctly?

A. I wanted to go, but, I had to clean the house.

B. We shoveled the snow, after the blizzard.

C. Yes, I bought a new car, with my savings.

D. It is chilly out, so I need a sweater.

38. Which sentence is written correctly?

A. The boy that lost his cat organized a search.

B. The student whom I helped study got an A.

C. I like the actor which played the thief.

D. Who will you go with?

39. Which sentence is written correctly?

A. The article I wrote is titled "Famous Speeches in America."

B. Thomas Jefferson wrote *the Declaration of Independence*.

C. My friend got a job at the "Miami Herald" newspaper.

D. *The Monkey's Paw* is a short story that students often read.

40. Read the paragraph.

> Scientists measure earthquakes using a seismometer, which records the movement of the ground. They use a Richter scale of 1–10 to describe the severity of the quake. If a quake measures a 6, it is 10 times bigger than one that measures a 5.

This paragraph is missing an introduction. Which is the best introduction for this paragraph?

A. Earthquakes occur when the tectonic plates that make up the Earth's crust and upper mantle move.

B. Smaller quakes called aftershocks follow a big quake.

C. Earthquakes can be very scary and people usually get no warning.

D. If you live where there are earthquakes, you should have an emergency kit.

41. Read the paragraph.

> (1) The men have their soccer tournament this weekend. (2) The women have one, to, but it is a week later. (3) You're welcome to come watch with us. (4) They're expected to do very well.

Which sentence is *not* written correctly?

A. 1

B. 2

C. 3

D. 4

42. Which sentence is written correctly?

A. Please, "restart your computer," the technician said.

B. "Your blood test results look great" the nurse said.

C. The chef said, "Add the mushrooms once the onions are soft."

D. The landscaper asked if "I wanted more flowers."

43. Read the sentences.

> You do not have to do anything to turn on the alarm. It is automatic.

What does the word *automatic* mean?

A. working by itself

B. on a timer

C. a smart sensor

D. wireless

44. Read the paragraph.

> Remodeling your kitchen can be exciting, especially if you like to cook. You can pick your appliances and get more counter space. _____, it can be stressful. Where do you eat while the kitchen is under construction?

The paragraph is missing a relationship word. Which is the best choice?

A. In addition

B. Moreover

C. However

D. As a result

45. Which sentence is written correctly?

    A. Mo said he can be able to go to the game if he finishes painting.

    B. Nyala may definitely get the job because of her great interview.

    C. Lawrence must call the bank if he wants to.

    D. Rhiannon may try to sell her car.

46. Read the paragraph.

(1) When you have a job interview, you need to prepare. (2) It is a good idea to find out as much about the place where you are interviewing as possible. (3) A simple step is to look on the company's website. (4) Then, try to think of questions you might be asked, and come up with answers ahead of time. (5) Don't forget that you should wear business clothes even if the company is more casual. (6) These steps will give you a better chance of getting the job.

Read the sentence.

You should find and understand the company's philosophy and business practices.

What is the best place to add the following sentence?

    A. after Sentence 2

    B. after Sentence 3

    C. after Sentence 4

    D. after Sentence 5

47. Which sentence is written correctly?

    A. Today in class we read chapters, 4, 5, and 6.

    B. Yes we will play in the snow, but after it stops.

    C. Before the next storm, I need to buy new boots.

    D. Micaela, loves camping, because the air smells so fresh.

48. Read the paragraph.

(1) After I work out. (2) I am sore and sweaty, but feel like I did something good. (3) I go home and take a long, hot shower. (4) Then, I make sure I eat protein and drink plenty of water.

Which sentence is *not* written correctly?

    A. 1

    B. 2

    C. 3

    D. 4

49. Which sentence is written correctly?

    A. The Cities the tour bus stopped in are Boston, New York, Philadelphia, and Washington, D.C.

    B. The Coach says I am a good athlete, because I won a Golf Trophy.

    C. My daughter is going to school to be a dentist.

    D. Marcus is the President of the town's charity association.

50. Read the paragraph.

In most places on Earth except on the equator, days and nights change length throughout the year. You will experience days and nights that are almost equal lengths when there is an equinox. They are the first day of spring and fall. _____, the longest day of the year is the first day of summer. The shortest day is the first day of winter.

The paragraph is missing a relationship word. Which is the best choice?

    A. Furthermore

    B. Otherwise

    C. Because

    D. As a result

Answers begin on page 110.

TABE Practice Test Action Plan

Highlight all the questions that you answered correctly. Count the number of correct answers and write that in the second column. The results will help identify the skills that need improvement.

Questions	Number Correct	Skills	Pages
8, 9, 48	_____ / 3	Write Complete Sentences	16–17
11, 38	_____ / 2	Use Relative Pronouns and Adverbs	18
17, 41	_____ / 2	Use Frequently Confused Words	18–19
5, 31	_____ / 2	Use Conjunctions, Prepositions, and Interjections	23–25
3, 33, 45	_____ / 3	Form Verb Tenses	25–27
21, 36, 49	_____ / 3	Capitalize Correctly	33
22, 39	_____ / 2	Write Titles of Works	33–34
2, 28	_____ / 2	Spell Correctly	34–35
23, 37, 47	_____ / 3	Use Commas	39–41
7, 35, 42	_____ / 3	Punctuate Quotations	41
16, 32	_____ / 2	Modify Sentences	45–46
15, 34	_____ / 2	Identify Dialects in Fiction	47–48
1, 30, 43	_____ / 3	Determine Definitions	59–61
18 ,19, 20	_____ / 3	Use Topic Words	65–66
13, 27, 44, 50	_____ / 4	Use Relationship Words	71
6, 12, 29	_____ / 3	Write Opinion Pieces	79–80
4, 24, 40	_____ / 3	Introduce Informative/Explanatory Texts	85
10, 14, 25, 26, 46	_____ / 5	Write Informative/Explanatory Texts	86–87
Total	_____ **/ 50**		

Answer Key

Pretest

1. **B.** The correlative conjunction for *neither* is *nor*. *Neither* means not either.

2. **D.** The first sentence introduces the topic of the galaxy and places us in it. The next sentence introduces the idea of stars. The next gives background for the reader, and the final sentence introduces the topic of galaxy research.

3. **A.** The past participle is usually the *–ed* form of the verb.

4. **C.** *Mom* is capitalized only when used as a proper noun. *Doctor* is capitalized when used as a title before a name.

5. **C.** The sentence is informal and does not support the topic.

6. **A.** The word is spelled *accommodate*.

7. **A.** The statement is an opinion because many people without college educations are successful.

8. **C.** Quotes are introduced with a comma, begin with a capital letter, and have the punctuation mark before the end quotation mark.

9. **C.** Formal style avoids slang and contractions and is specific.

10. **A.** Use a comma between independent clauses when they are combined in one sentence by a coordinating conjunction.

11. **D.** The sentence states the topic and does not offer an opinion.

12. **B.** *Chronology* comes from the Greek root *chrono*, which means time, and *logy*, which means the study of. The context cue is timeline.

13. **C.** The word *therefore* signals a result.

14. **B.** The sentence contains an independent clause made up of a subject and a verb.

15. **A.** The paragraph has a topic sentence and a logical order of action items. The last sentence is a conclusion to the topic.

16. **C.** The relative pronoun *that* refers to animals or things, not people. *Who* would be the correct pronoun to use in this sentence.

17. **C.** The sentence uses academic language to introduce the essay's ideas.

18. **D.** *You're* is a contraction for you are.

19. **A.** The sentence sets the context and tells the reader what to expect.

20. **C.** Commas indicate direct address and separate items in a list.

21. **B.** The quote supports the idea that practice is required to be good at playing an instrument.

22. **B.** Arachnids, such as spiders, have eight legs. Insects have six.

23. **C.** A *segment* is a part of an arachnid or insect body.

24. **A.** *Antennae* are thin, wiry parts that insects have, but arachnids don't.

25. **A.** *Y'all* is a regional word used for the plural of you.

26. **D.** Book titles are italicized in text.

27. **D.** The sentence contains a subject and a verb, the two elements necessary for a complete sentence.

28. **C.** The sentence offers a second reason to travel by airplane.

29. **A.** The sentence gives a reason that reading literature is important.

30. **D.** *Must* is a modal auxiliary that is used with another verb to convey necessity.

31. **B.** In the sentence, *for his advice* is a prepositional phrase.

32. **D.** Capitalize geographical references and titles when used as a direct address.

33. **A.** Both *privilege* and *occasion* are spelled correctly.

34. **B.** The statement builds the argument that soccer is the world's most popular sport by offering a fact to back it up.

35. **A.** Place a comma after introductory elements.

36. **A.** Formal language avoids contractions and is more precise.

37. **B.** The prefix *dys* means bad or difficult and the root *graph* means write.

38. **C.** The two sentences, "The letters, or notes, are written on a staff. The staff has five lines" give the answer.

39. **A.** *Nevertheless* shows that the second statement is in contrast to the first statement.

40. **B.** The word *however* shows contrast.

41. **C.** No comma is needed if the signal phrase ends with an exclamation point.

42. **C.** Book titles are italicized.

43. **C.** A sentence explaining why tsunamis are dangerous is the most logical addition because the paragraph mentions that they are dangerous, but does not say why.

44. **B.** The words *had been walking* indicate past perfect tense.

45. **D.** The word *on* is the correct preposition for the phrase *on her nose*.

46. **D.** The commonly confused words *there* and *your* are used correctly in this sentence.

47. **A.** The sentence has a clear opinion that can be backed up with logical reasons.

48. **A.** The word *pop* is dialect for *soda* in some parts of the United States.

49. **A.** The subject pronoun *who* is used for people.

50. **C.** An introduction should orient the reader to the topic and include a clear topic sentence.

Unit 1

Lesson 1

2. **A.** A comma alone cannot combine two independent clauses. The other options avoid a run-on by either combining the clauses (with a semicolon or a comma and conjunction) or by creating two sentences.

3. **C.** This choice contains a subject and predicate. The other choices are missing one or the other. They are sentence fragments.

4. **D.** This proper order here is quantity (*three*), size (*large*), age (*old*), shape (*round*), and material (*silk*).

5. **A.** The description *that don't bark* is essential for showing which dogs the speaker likes. Therefore, *that* should be used without commas.

6. **D.** The phrase *traveled to Spain* is essential to knowing which time the speaker is referring to. Therefore, *when* should be used without commas.

7. **B.** Choice A should use *ensure*. Choice C should use *break*. Choice D should use *through*.

8. **B.** *Such as welding, plumbing, and coding* does not contain a subject or a predicate. It should not appear as a full sentence.

9. **C.** One way to fix a run-on sentence is to divide it into two or more sentences. Choice D would be correct if the semicolon were a comma.

10. **D.** The correct order for this sentence is quantity (*several*), size (*large*), age (*new*), material (*iron*), and purpose (*support*).

11. **A, C, E.** Choice B is wrong because it implies that the manager doesn't like any workers and that all workers show up late. Choice D is wrong because it uses *that* instead of *who*.

12. **B.** In choice A, *they're*, *effects*, and *there* are wrong. In choice C, *except*, *effects*, and *there* are wrong. In choice D, *except*, *there*, and *their* are wrong.

Lesson 2

2. **A.** *Because* is the only conjunction in these sentences.

3. **B.** Choice A should be *neither . . . nor*, C should be *either . . . or*, and D should be *both . . . and*.

4. **D.** Only D contains a preposition (*in*) and a prepositional phrase (*in my car*).

5. **B.** The speaker doesn't know where Letricia is, so *might* is the best choice because it shows probability.

6. **A.** The past participle of *choose* is *chosen*. *Chose* is the simple past form of *choose*. *Choice* is a noun.

7. **C.** Choice A uses simple future tense (*will listen*). Choice B uses present perfect tense (*have listened*). Choice D uses simple past tense (*listened*).

8. **C.** Choice C has a conjunction (*or*), a preposition (*into*), and an interjection (*well*). Choices A and D do not have interjections. Choice B does not have a conjunction.

9. **A, B.** In choice C, *both . . . or* is wrong. In choice D, *yet* should be *but*.

10. **C.** Choice A is wrong because "We are going" is not a prepositional phrase. Although *to* can sometimes be a preposition, in Choice B it is part of the infinitive verb *to paint*. Choice D is wrong because "that house" is not a prepositional phrase and does not answer the question *When?*

11. **D.** Choices A and B are wrong because *have* is not a modal auxiliary. Choice C is wrong because *can* does not give a sense of obligation here. The workers are allowed, or permitted, to have up to 60 minutes for lunch.

12. **C.** "Had wrote" (in choice A) is always incorrect. The grammar in choice B is OK, but the sentence does not contain a past participle. "I written" (in choice D) is incorrect because a helping verb (*have/has/had*) is missing.

13. **A.** Choice B incorrectly uses present perfect. Choice C incorrectly uses past perfect. Choice D incorrectly uses simple past.

Lesson 3

2. **A.** In choice B, *Fall* should be *fall*. In choice C, *Uncle* should be *uncle*. In choice D, *Mayor* should be *mayor*.

3. **C.** Choice A is wrong because article names should be in quotation marks. Choice B is wrong because article names should not be italicized. Choice D is wrong because newspaper names should not have quotation marks.

4. **D.** In Choice A, the correct spelling is *specializes*. In Choice B, the correct spelling is *taxes*. In Choice C, the correct spelling is *taxes*.

5. **A.** In Choice B, *day* should be *Day*. In Choice C, *monday* should be *Monday*. In Choice D, *may* should be *May*.

6. **C.** In Choices A and B, the novel's title should be italicized. In Choice D, the author's name should not be italicized.

7. **D.** In Choice A, *shingels* should be *shingles*. In Choice B, *rooves* should be *roofs*. In Choice C, *shingels* should be *shingles* and *rooves* should be *roofs*.

8. **B.** In Choice A, *Eastern* should be *eastern*. In Choice C, *arabia* should be *Arabia*. In Choice D, *eid* should be *Eid*.

9. **A.** Choice B is wrong because *Cell Phones* should not be capitalized; the term is not a brand name. Choices C and D are wrong because *Company* should not be capitalized; it is not a brand name.

10. **A, C.** In Choice B, *Sports Illustrated* should be in italics with no quotation marks. In Choice D, *The Old Man and the Sea* should be in italics, and *Pulitzer Prize* should not. In Choice E, *Cosmopolitan* should be in italics.

11. **A.** Choice B is wrong because the plural of *belief* is *beliefs*. *Believe(s)* is a verb. Choice C is wrong because *handle* is the correct spelling. Choice D is wrong because the *h* in *handle* is not silent.

Lesson 4

2. **C.** Place a comma to set off the word *no* when it is the first word in a sentence in response to a question.

3. **A.** Place a comma after a long introductory phrase at the beginning of a sentence.

4. **C.** The items in the series are parsley, basil, and oregano. Commas should be placed after the first two items to separate them in the series.

5. **A.** Put a comma after a long introductory phrase at the beginning of a sentence.

6. **B.** Use a comma to separate the speaker from a direct quotation.

7. **B.** Place a comma before a coordinating conjunction that joins two independent clauses. The other answer choices place commas where they interrupt the flow of the sentences.

8. **B.** Place a comma before a coordinating conjunction that joins two independent clauses. Choice A does not need a comma; choice C is missing commas between the items in series; the comma in choice D interrupts the flow of the sentence.

9. **A.** Use a comma to separate the items in a series.

10. **B, C, D.** Choice B correctly includes a comma after a long introductory phrase. The comma in choice C sets off a question word at the end of the sentence. Choice D begins with a name, Pablo, which is a direct address and should be set off from the rest of the sentence.

11. **A.** Use a comma to set off *yes* or *no* from the rest of the sentence. Commas in the other choices all interrupt the flow of the sentences and do not follow any of the rules for using commas.

12. **D.** Use a comma to separate a direct quotation from the speaker by placing a comma at the end of the quote and inside the quotation marks.

Lesson 5

2. *Possible answer: I will not be able to attend tomorrow.* The phrase *gonna make it* is informal because it uses improper grammar.

3. *Possible answer: Annie purchased a new, expensive purse.* The verb *got* is informal because it is not very precise.

4. *Possible answer: What would you like to eat for lunch today?* The phrase *do you want* is informal because it is more casual, like something you might say to a close friend.

5. *Possible answer: George scheduled an appointment for next month.* The verb *made* is informal because it is not very precise.

6. **B.** The other options use full, long words like *received*, *apologize*, and *availability*. You probably wouldn't use these in a casual conversation.

7. **A, C.** The important connection between the two sentences is that they contradict. The conjunctions *but* and *although* show this.

8. **D.** Although the first three sentences combine more than one idea, they are clearer and smoother to read than Sentence 4.

9. **D.** *You betcha* is a phrase meaning *You bet* in certain regions of the U.S.

10. **D.** The phrase *will be out of the office* is clear and precise. It does not use contractions or slang.

11. **B.** Although all of the options are grammatically correct, option B expresses all of the facts in the shortest and clearest way.

12. **C.** Option C is short and simple. It focuses on the quick connection between Greta smelling the pie and Greta remembering her grandmother.

13. **B, D.** When writing to a teacher, it's best to use more formal language. This includes using full and precise words and phrases.

14. **C.** The phrase *What d'ye* is used to mean *What do you* in some regions.

15. **A.** The passage shows an example of a formal letter. The register refers to the level of formality of the language.

16. **A, D, E.** Informal language is more casual. It uses slang, abbreviations, and contractions.

Unit 1 Skill Check

1. **D.** The predicate contains the main verb in the sentence and usually all the words following the main verb.

2. **My friend has two well-behaved, tiny, black and white Dalmatian puppies.** The correct order for several adjectives in a sentence is: quantity, opinion, size, age, shape, color, origin, material, and purpose.

3. **A.** In the sentence, the clause "who works at the coffee shop" is nonessential information. With relative pronouns (such as *who*), a nonessential clause should have commas around it.

4. *Incorrect words: threw, break, Its.* Correct replacements: *through, brake, It's.* All of these word pairs are homophones, meaning that they sound exactly the same, but they have different meanings.

5. **C.** A preposition is a word that gives more information about something, like time or location. In C, the preposition is *at.*

6. **A.** Correlative conjunctions are made up of two or more words used together to connect parts of a sentence, like *both . . . and.*

7. **B, C, D.** These options use the modal auxiliaries *can* (expressing ability), *might* (expressing probability), and *Can* (expressing a request).

8. **D.** The word *see* has irregular past participles that need to be memorized.

9. **B.** The present progressive verb tense expresses a current action in progress.

10. My <u>birthday</u> is in June. Every year, I take a weekend trip around that time. This year, my <u>sister</u> and I will leave on a <u>Friday</u> to drive to <u>Lake</u> Michigan. I love going to the beach in the summer!

11. **B.** The titles of newspapers should be italicized. The titles of articles should be in quotation marks.

12. **C.** For a word that has a consonant directly before the *y,* as in *canary,* change the *y* to *i* and add *es* (*canaries*). The other correct pairs would be *fox / foxes, wolf / wolves,* and *sheep / sheep.*

13. **D.** The spelling error is *channle,* which should be *channel.* Many words that end in *le* or *el* are commonly misspelled.

14. A comma should follow each underlined word: Congress chose the District of Columbia to be the capital of the United States government in 1790. Congress first met in Washington, D.C., in <u>1800</u>, although construction on the first phase of the Capitol was not done until 1826. Moving forward in time to <u>today</u>, millions of people visit Washington, D.C., to see the <u>Capitol</u>, the White <u>House</u>, the Library of <u>Congress</u>, and many other monuments.

    Commas are used to separate clauses in compound sentences, as in the second sentence. They are used to set off long introductory phrases, as in the last sentence. They are also used to separate items in a series, as in the last sentence.

15. **A.** Commas are used to set off long phrases at the start of sentences, like in A.

16. **C.** Commas are used to set off specific words including: a person who is directly addressed (A and D), *yes* or *no* at the start of a sentence (B), and question words at the end of the sentence (C). C is the only option that shows a comma separating those words from the rest of the sentence.

17. **A.** For direct quotations, a comma should be placed between the speaker and the speaker's words.

18. **B.** While the other sentences are grammatically correct, B is the best option because it is shorter, clearer, and more concise.

19. *Possible answer: In the winter I like to sit by the fireplace, drink hot chocolate, and read a good book.*

20. **C.** Contractions and abbreviations may be used in certain dialects, but a dialect is a way of speaking.

21. **D.** D is the most formal because it is the most precise, and it uses correct grammar and avoids contractions.

Unit 2

Lesson 1

2. **A.** Choices B and C are wrong because *bio-* is not a prefix or a suffix. Choice D is wrong because *-graphy* is not a suffix.

3. **C.** Choice A has an explanation-type context clue. Choice B is a comparison-type context clue. Choice D is a contrast-type context clue.

4. **C.** A thesaurus groups together words with similar meanings.

5. **B.** The context gives clues about the meaning of the term *aphorism.*

6. **D.** The sentence gives this example of an aphorism: "A jack of all trades is master of none."

7. **D.** Choice A contains the root *graph*, which is related to *writing*. Choice B contains the root *viv*, which is related to *life*. Choice C contains the root *nov*, which is related to *new*.

8. **C.** The word *carcasses* is associated with dead or decaying flesh. It is a context clue. Another context clue is the contrast between *vibrant animals* and *carrion*. The word *instead* is used to show this contrast.

9. **A.** Choice A uses an antonym, *commended*, and a word that is the opposite of *dishonest*.

10. **C.** A *lingua franca* can be any common language used for communication among people who have different first languages.

Lesson 2

2. **Renaissance, world history**

3. **theory, crust, continental drift, plate tectonics**

4. **aquarium, ecosystem**

5. **supplemental restraint system**

6. **hieroglyphics, pyramid, ancient Egyptian**

7. **B.** The *premium* is the total amount paid for the insurance coverage.

8. **D.** A *policy* is a document that lists the type and amount of coverage provided by an insurance company.

9. **A.** The *deductible* is the amount that the insured person must pay each time he files an insurance claim.

Lesson 3

2. **but** This shows contrast between the time and money spent on the trip and the great beauty that the writer found in Hawaii.

3. **Although** The correct answer must show contrast between the people who know that exercise is important and those who exercise. The other two choices do not show contrast.

4. **nevertheless** *Nevertheless* shows that opposite relationship between her safe driving and her lateness.

5. **because** This shows effect. Tara was hungry and the effect of that hunger was her eating dinner.

6. **also** This sentence shows *how* Fernando is a singer as well as an actor.

7. **however** The contrast is between wanting to loan money and having money in the bank.

8. **A.** This choice shows the contrast between the rewarding and costly parts of owning a dog.

9. **B.** The two sentences name several things that you might have when you own a dog. Some are needed and the second sentence names additional things that you might buy.

10. **B.** This is the only answer choice that shows contrast between spending a lot of money and the love that a dog will pay you back.

11. **C.** This sentence shows the correct cause and effect relationship between leaving the party at 11 and the last train leaving at midnight. Choice A is an incomplete sentence; choice B shows an incorrect relationship; choice D uses two relationship words that do not make sense together.

12. **A.** This choice shows the correct contrast relationship. He did not go back to school and would not be able to get a better job. Choice B shows effect; choice C shows addition; choice D shows addition.

Unit 2 Skill Check

1. **C.** The sentences show a comparison-type context clue. You can guess that "scrupulous" is similar to basing your actions on what you think is right.

2. **A.** B is an example of a comparison-type context clue. C is an example-type context clue. D is an explanation-type context clue.

3. **D.** Suffixes are found at the end of the word. The suffix -*able* means *able* or *capable*.

4. **C.** The prefix of the word *aquatic* is *aqua-*, which relates to water. Although B relates to water, *aqua* is not specific to *fins*.

5. **B.** A thesaurus provides synonyms for words.

6. **Topic words:** *fault lines, seismic waves, epicenter, seismographs.* These topic words are all specific to the subject of earthquakes.

7. **D.** Based on the context of the paragraph, the word *altitude* refers to height. Option D uses the word to mean height.

8. **B.** Based on the context of the sentence, *export* refers to sending goods out of a place. Option B describes growing and selling resources to other places.

9. **D.** The paragraph describes the different parts of atoms. Even though it uses other topic words, they all relate to atoms.

10. **D.** We know from the paragraph that protons are positively charged particles. Electrons are negative, and neutrons have no charge. They are all building blocks of atoms but are located in different places. Based on all of this, *pro-* most likely means *positive*.

11. **Topic words:** *matter, protons, neutrons, electrons, nucleus, shells, orbitals.* The topic words are all specific to the subject of atoms.

12. **Relationship words:** *in addition to, furthermore, although.* Relationship words connect pieces of information. In the paragraph, the phrases *in addition to, furthermore,* and *although* each connect two different ideas.

13. **The two ideas:** Daria dropped her cell phone and had to pay for the screen to be repaired. The relationship words *as a result* show that Daria dropping her cell phone is what caused her to pay for the repair.

14. **D.** The idea that painting by yourself can take time and effort is being contrasted with the idea that it can save you money. Therefore, *but* is the best relationship word to use.

15. **A.** From the sentence, you can tell that the strong winds caused the napkins to blow away. The phrase *due to* shows cause.

16. **C.** The two ideas of the sentence are *that I was really nervous* and *that I went through with it.* These ideas show contrast, so *nevertheless* works correctly. The other sentences link through cause or addition, which do not correctly show the contrast.

Unit 3

Lesson 1

3. **C.** The writer's opinion is that Picasso was the greatest artist of his time. This sentence supports that opinion with a reason. The phrase *in particular* helps link the opinion with the reason.

4. **D.** The phrase *once again* is a clue that this is a paraphrase that is part of the conclusion.

5. **A.** This is a statement of fact, so it cannot be an opinion or conclusion. It introduces the topic of hiking.

6. **C.** Section 2 has a topic sentence followed by an opinion. Sections 3 and 4 have reasons. Section 1 paraphrases the original opinion. It also adds a reason.

7. **C.** Section 4 discusses the damage the Asian carp cause. Section 3 discusses how Asian carp can injure people. The word *too* connects these ideas so it must be placed between them.

8. **B.** Choice A is not the topic. Choice C is the main opinion. Choice D is part of the piece, but not the topic.

9. **C.** Choice A is not the writer's opinion. Choice B is the topic. Choice D is part of the piece, but not the main opinion.

10. **C.** Choices A, B, and D present other ideas. They do not paraphrase the original opinion.

11. **A.** Choices B, C, and D present other ideas. They are not supporting reasons.

12. **D.** Choices A, B, and C are opinions.

Lesson 2

2. **D.** Choice A is wrong because a conclusion would not state what the article will discuss. Choices B and C are wrong because the sentence offers no support for anything.

3. **C.** *First* shows that this is the beginning of a list of steps.

4. **B.** The word *permethrin* is specific medication and insecticide.

5. **D.** *20% DEET* is a very specific, or concrete, detail.

6. **A.** This sentence doesn't have enough information for it to be a kind of support. That means B and D are wrong. And there is no domain-specific vocabulary.

7. **D.** The quotation marks show that this is a supporting quote.

8. **A.** The topic should be stated in the first paragraph. This rules out choices B, C, and D.

9. **B, C, D.** Tubman was born into slavery. This gives context. But it does not support the claim that she was an important figure in American history.

10. **B.** *Abolitionist* and *suffragette* are academic words.

11. **C.** Choice C is the only one that summarizes the topic.

Unit 3 Skill Check

1. **C.** The sentence introduces the topic and states a clear opinion.

2. **A.** *Consequently* is a transition word that shows the effect or result of an action.

3. **B.** The sentence reminds the reader of the opinion stated in the topic sentence.

4. *Early morning high school start times can be tough on teenagers. Studies show teenagers need more sleep. Their body clocks are set to a nighttime schedule. Therefore, high school students should never have to start school before 9 a.m.* The paragraph introduces a topic, gives two logical reasons, and states an opinion based on the reasons.

5. **A.** *Therefore* is a transition word that shows a result or gives a logical next step.

6. **C.** The statement supports the opinion by giving a strong reason why it is important to hire a trained worker.

7. **A.** The statement is an opinion. Although it is true that cellphones can be distracting, not every person would agree with this statement.

8. *Travel can be very rewarding. You get a change of scenery. Secondly, you can learn about other cultures. Also, it can be very relaxing. Everyone should try to travel at least once a year.* The paragraph introduces the topic, uses introductory words to offer reasons, and ends with an opinion statement.

9. **D.** The statement uses specific biological language to introduce the topic of genetics.

10. **B.** The statement is an important fact about the history of written language.

11. **C.** A good conclusion wraps up the topic with an inference or generalization that puts together all the facts in the essay.

12. **C.** The sentence gives an overview of the topic of the essay.

13. **A.** The quotation gives an example of an artist painting in order to express feelings.

14. **A.** The paragraph does not define *algorithm*; therefore, a reader might not understand what the author means.

15. **D.** The main idea of the paragraph is that anyone can run a marathon if they have dedication and some training.

TABE Test Practice

1. **A.** The root *photo* means *light* and to *synthesize* is to *combine*.

2. **B.** The word *rhythm* is spelled correctly.

3. **C.** The present perfect tense *happening* shows an action is ongoing in the present.

4. **B.** The introduction orients the reader and clearly introduces the topic.

5. **B.** The correlative conjunctions *both* and *and* are used in a pair.

6. **D.** The sentence is supported by reason and paraphrases the point of view.

7. **C.** Place a comma after the signal phrase if it interrupts a direct quotation.

8. **C.** A complete sentence has a one subject and a predicate.

9. **A.** Adjectives should be added in this order: quantity, opinion, size, age, shape, color, origin, material, and purpose. No comma is needed after the quantity.

10. **B.** The sentence gives a concrete detail that adds to information about roses and water.

11. **B.** The adverb *why* shows reason.

12. **A.** The conclusion restates the opinion of the writer.

13. **A.** The word *furthermore* signals additional information.

14. **D.** The sentence gives a concrete detail about the suggestion before it.

15. **B.** The sentence includes the phrase *concrete jungle* for city and *ain't*.

16. **A.** This sentence avoids contractions, slang, uses correct grammar, and is precise.

17. **C.** The contraction *they're* is short for *they are*. The word *your* shows possession.

18. **A.** The last sentence explains that a level helps a carpenter tell whether something is slanted or not. Go back to the paragraph to check the definition if you are unsure.

19. **A.** The paragraph states that a nail gun saves time and energy when pounding many nails. Go back to the paragraph to check the definition if you are unsure.

20. **C.** The paragraph states that a saw is used to cut wood. Go back to the paragraph to check the definition if you are unsure.

21. **B.** Names of holidays are capitalized.

22. **C.** Titles of works such as book, journals, newspapers, websites, stories, poems, articles, and plays should be italicized.

23. **B.** Place a comma to set off words such as *yes* and *no*, and after introductory elements such as *after I eat dinner.*

24. **D.** The introduction to an informative/explanatory text should introduce the topic clearly with precise language.

25. **D.** The sentence gives a detail about the topic, which is the number of bones in the human body.

26. **D.** The rest of the paragraph in about the topic of the sinking of the Titanic and Margaret Brown's part in saving people.

27. **D.** The word *similar* signals a comparison.

28. **D.** The words *definitely* and *appearance* are spelled correctly.

29. **A.** The conclusion paraphrases the point of view.

30. **D.** The word *capsize* means to overturn or tip over. The rocking of the boat is a context clue.

31. **B.** A prepositional phrase consists of a preposition, its object, and any words that modify the object.

32. **C.** Formal writing avoids slang and contractions. It uses precise language.

33. **B.** The word *went* is past tense. The rest of the paragraph discusses the future.

34. **A.** Dialect uses different words to express the same thing. The words *fixing to put the book up* mean *planning to put the book away*.

35. **A.** Place a comma after a signal phrase if it interrupts the quotation.

36. **C.** Places such as states are capitalized.

37. **D.** Place a comma before coordinating conjunctions such as *so* to separate independent clauses.

38. **B.** The word *whom* is a direct object used for a person.

39. **A.** Place quotation marks around titles of articles, chapters, and stories.

40. **A.** The sentence introduces the topic and includes domain-specific language.

41. **B.** The word *to* indicates direction. The word *too* means also.

42. **C.** Place a comma after the signal phrase if the signal phrase is before the quotation.

43. **A.** The prefix *auto-* means *self*.

44. **C.** The word *however* signals a contrast.

45. **D.** The word *may* signals permission, possibility, or uncertainty.

46. **B.** The sentence adds the detail about why you should look on the company's website, which is mentioned in Sentence 3.

47. **C.** Place a comma after introductory elements.

48. **A.** The words *after I work out* make up a prepositional phrase. A complete sentence needs a subject and a verb.

49. **C.** The word *dentist* is only capitalized when used as a title.

50. **A.** The word *furthermore* signals additional information.

Glossary

abbreviation shortened form of a word or phrase (examples: feat. for featuring, ed. for edition, acct. for account)

affix word part that gets attached to the beginning or end of a root word to change its meaning

capitalization the act of putting a capital letter at the start of a word

comparison showing how two or more things are alike

complete sentence a sentence that includes a complete thought. It begins with a capital letter, ends with a punctuation mark, and contains a subject (whether actual or understood) and a predicate (including a verb).

compound sentence a sentence with two or more independent clauses

conclusion the end part of a written piece

concrete details specific, rather than general, information

conjunction a word that connects sentences, clauses, phrases, or words

context clues information that appears near an unknown word or phrase that can help readers understand the unknown text

contraction a shortened word formed by combining two words and replacing letters with an apostrophe (examples: *isn't, hasn't, they're, we're, you're, we'll, you'll, he's, she's, it's*)

contrast showing how two or more things are different

coordinating conjunction a word like *and*, *but*, and *or* that separates two independent clauses in one sentence. Both clauses are equally important and neither is dependent on the other.

dialect a way of speaking that is particular to a specific area

direct quotation the exact words spoken by someone or copied from a printed work

domain-specific language words used mainly within a certain field of study or line of work

fragment a group of words that looks like a sentence but does not contain both a subject and a predicate

generalization a general statement about a broad category of things

independent clause a group of words which has a subject and a verb and can stand alone as a complete sentence

inference a conclusion or opinion that can be formed from given information

interjection a word, phrase, or sound that expresses sudden or strong feeling

introduction the beginning part of a book, essay, or other written piece that explains what will follow in the main part

italics a slanted style of type

logical sensible; reasonable

misspelled spelled wrong

modal auxiliary verb used with another verb to express a mood or tense

predicate the part of a sentence that contains a verb and states something about the sentence's subject

preposition a word or group of words that is used with a noun, pronoun, or noun phrase to show direction, location, or time, or to introduce an object

quotation marks punctuation marks used to set off exact words or a title

reference material a source of information or facts

register the level of formality in language

relationship words words that show connections between words or ideas

relative adverb one of a set of adverbs (*when*, *where*, or *why*) used to provide more information about a subject

relative pronoun one of a set of pronouns (*who*, *whom*, *whose*, *that*, or *which*) used to provide more information about a subject

root the main part of a word

run-on sentence a group of words that looks like a sentence but contains two or more independent clauses that are not properly connected with a word or punctuation

slang informal, nonstandard words and phrases used by a particular group of people

subject the main noun or pronoun in a sentence that is connected to the main verb in a sentence

topic word word related to a specific subject